Earn College Credit For What You Know

Earn College Credit For What You Know

Susan Simosko

ACROPOLIS BOOKS LTD.

ACROPOLIS BOOKS LTD.
11250-22 Roger Bacon Dr.
Reston, VA 22090

Library of Congress Cataloging in Publication Data

Simosko, Susan, 1942-
  How to earn college credit for what you know.

   1. College credits—United States—Outside work—
Evaluation. 2. Nonformal education—United States—
Evaluation. 3. Independent study—United States—
Evaluation. 4. Equivalency tests—United States.
I. Title.
LB2360.S65   1985   378.168   84-24544
ISBN 0-87491-773-5 (pbk.)

 42

ATTENTION: Schools and Corporations

ACROPOLIS books are available at quantity discounts with bulk purchase for educational, business, or sales
promotional use. For information, please write to: SPECIAL SALES DEPARTMENT, ACROPOLIS BOOKS LTD.,
11250-22 Roger Bacon Dr., Reston, VA 22090.

For my mother, father, and my daughter, Nina,
each of whom knows the value of
learning from experience.

Acknowledgments

I would like to express my sincere gratitude to the staff of Vermont State Colleges for granting me permission to use material from *Earning College Credit for Prior Experiential Learning, A Student Handbook on Educational Assessment and Portfolio Preparation,* a publication of the Office of External Programs, Vermont State College, Waterbury, Vermont.

I am also grateful to the administration of Thomas A. Edison State College for permitting me to use material from *Earning College Credit for What You Know: A Student Handbook in Portfolio Assessment* and to the staff who contributed so much to the preparation and subsequent revisions of that publication.

Special thanks must be extended to Aubrey Forrest, E. Sharon Hayenga, Laura Adams, Norma Rowe, Ruth Cargo, and Valerie McIntyre for their contributions to various CAEL publications, from which material has been adapted for inclusion in this book.

Heartfelt thanks go out to Morris Keeton for inviting me to write this book and for his inspirational mentoring.

I would also like to extend my deepest appreciation to Robin Hendrickson for her saint-like patience in typing the several drafts and final manuscript.

Lastly, I would like to thank my colleagues at Edison State College, Diane E. Gruenberg and Paul I. Jacobs, for their thoughtful reviews of this manuscript, their helpful comments and sustaining support.

Susan Simosko

Table of Contents

3.

Documenting What You Know and Can Do 61

4.

Organizing Your Portfolio 75

5.

Bringing It All Together 89

6.

Postscript: An Adult Guide to Understanding Colleges 95

Appendix A

Addresses of Testing Organizations   **117**

Appendix B

Introduction to Writing Samples   **119**

Appendix C

Sample Forms for Your Portfolio   **135**

List of Institutions   **141**

Experience
Teaches

— Tacitus

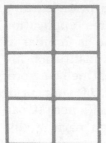

Prologue

At colleges and universities all across the United States, you can earn credit for college-level learning and skills you already possess. The key to your success will be to demonstrate to experts in the field that you really do possess the knowledge and skills you claim to have. One method of demonstrating your knowledge and competence is through a process called the assessment of prior learning or portfolio assessment.*

To earn college credit through a prior learning assessment program, you will draw upon the rich learning experiences obtained from your employment, community service activities, your independent reading, non-collegiate courses and training, or your own special interests and accomplishments. As you undergo the assessment process, the knowledge and skills you have obtained will be equated to the learning that takes place in college classrooms. The purposes of this book are to help you:

1. consider your life and educational goals,

2. explore your own background as you consider the assessment options available to you,

3. prepare the best possible documentation or evidence to support your learning claim, and

4. consider your assessment plan in light of your broader educational goals.

---

* Frequently, the terms "assessment of prior learning" and "portfolio assessment" are used interchangeably. Strictly speaking, however, it is your knowledge and skills, *not* your portfolio that is assessed. As will be discussed throughout this book, the function of the portfolio is to document what you know and can do.

Undoubtedly your own institution, if it has a prior learning assessment program, will have its own brochures, application forms, fees, and procedures. You will want to be as familiar as possible with these so that both you and your institution are clear about your educational plans and progress. One last word: Earning college-credit through an assessment of your prior learning can be an exciting and rewarding experience. It can also save you valuable time and money as you earn credits without sitting through classes to learn what you already know. Last but not least, it can be fun. We hope this book contributes in all these ways to prior learning assessment experience and to your success.

Sandy began her career as a secretary and is now head of the word processing department in her company. In addition to the 18 credit hours she earned for her knowledge of typing, shorthand and secretarial procedures, she earned six more credits for word processing and word processing management. Sandy does creative writing in her leisure time and has had several poems published. As a result of this accomplishment, she earned an additional nine credits in creative writing and poetry.

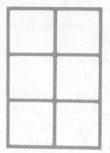

Introduction

*I have but one lamp by which my
feet are guided, and that is the
lamp of experience.*

—Patrick Henry

As you begin to think about starting the assessment process, keep in mind that you are joining the ranks of thousands of adult students who are entering for the first time or re-entering college programs throughout the United States. During the last twenty years, students over the age of 25 have become the fastest growing group of the entire college population. In 1981, the *Chronicle of Higher Education* reported that one of every three college students was over 25 years of age.

Needless to say, colleges and universities have modified or implemented new programs to respond to the changing needs of their new student body. They have dramatically increased the number of external degree programs, credit-by-examination opportunities, flexible course schedules, evening programs, work-study programs, non-credit courses and weekend colleges, to provide increased flexibility, opportunity, and access to higher education by adults.*

---

* For a fuller discussion on how to select the best college for you, turn to the Postscript: "Adult Guide to Understanding Colleges." You will also want to review the list of colleges found at the end of this book, each of which has policies for recognizing prior learning.

Although this book will help you through the prior learning assessment process, consider also some of the other opportunities available to you for earning college credit. Some may be easier for you than portfolio assessment, more appropriate, less expensive, or more in keeping with your educational plans. Whatever the reason, or the combination of reasons, you should explore *all* of the options. Never before in the history of the United States have there been so many flexible opportunities for adults wanting or needing college credit or a degree. Don't hesitate to draw upon all the resources you can!

Looking at your Life and Educational Objectives

Many excellent, insightful books have been written on the various stages of adult development, but few of us go around believing that our problems or situations are solely the result of a "developmental stage." While we might attribute a young child's rambunctiousness to the "Terrible Two's," we don't usually analyze our adult lives in this way. And for good reason. Each of us has a unique set of background experiences, values, relationships, goals, and resources that don't seem to fall together like anyone else's we know. Of course we see similarities with others and may share common interests, activities, religious affiliations, or aspirations. In almost every case, however, after we are done exploring the similarities, we say, "But I'm different. My life went in *this* direction, I chose *this* profession, I decided to marry *this* person," and so forth. Our sense of uniqueness is probably the single most common factor we share with human beings everywhere on the globe!

Just as no two faces or sets of fingerprints are exactly the same, so, too, each of us, in the very deepest sense, is unlike anyone else on the planet. We are complex, separate individuals continually trying to make a place for ourselves in a complex, changing world—one that places heavy demands on us emotionally, intellectually, socially, economically, and often physically. Changing the course of one's life, then, is no simple matter. But it is often necessary. Not so many years ago, the average expected age of our forefathers was 40. Now the average man or woman can expect to live well beyond 70. Is it any wonder that we find people making two, three or even four major changes in their lives? Careers change, family situations change, life-styles move in new directions. We frequently read about these transitions in our magazines and novels, and certainly the television and film industries have thrived in depicting change in individuals, families or society as a whole.

What, you may be wondering, does all of this have to do with me and my desire to earn college credit? The answer is quite simple. Professionals in the field of adult education, and many individuals who have made significant changes in their lives through continuing their educations have found that if you are specific in your life goals, you are well on your way to making the specific educational plans to reach those goals. Few of us would be likely to commit large amounts of time, money or energy to a project or activity that did not have some significance or value to us. To the extent possible, each of us seeks to integrate who we are now with who we will be in the future.

Most of the activities you will be doing in conjunction with the assessment of your prior learning as discussed in this *Book* will focus on your past: looking at what you've already done or learned that has helped you acquire college-level knowledge. But at this early stage, you will want to think about your future: what do you want to be doing in five years? Ten years? Do you want to enter a new vocation or profession? Do you want to increase your competence in a skill you already have? Do you want to find a solution to a serious social or environmental problem? Do you want to enrich your retirement years? Do you want to acquire credentials for professional advancement? Do you want to change your routine and learn something entirely new?

Answering these and other questions about your future will help you map out your *educational objectives.*

1. Do you need to complete a degree?
2. Do you need to learn more about a particular field?
3. Do you need to prepare for a licensing or certifying exam?
4. Do you want to qualify for a different line of work?
5. Do you need to get admitted to graduate school?
6. Do you want to complete something you began several years ago?

Consider the lives of the two individuals described below to help you think about your own particular life and educational objectives.

Jim is 42. He is sales manager of a retail company that sells camping equipment. After high school, Jim decided to wait a year or two before beginning college in order to learn something about himself—like what he wanted to do with his life—and earn money. He got a job as a salesman and discovered that he was successful and well-liked by both his customers and his supervisors. Even more than that, he really enjoyed selling.

After working for several different firms as a salesman, Jim applied for his current position five years ago. He was very pleased with himself for getting the job, since the ad in the newspaper had specified "college degree helpful." Although Jim knows the company is happy with his work—he has gotten several bonuses in addition to regular raises—he has been passed over for several assistant vice president positions and knows that is the next step in his career. He also knows that he could handle the work.

Over the years, Jim has been involved with a local service organization and served for several years on the Board of Directors of his local YMCA. A few years ago when his younger child was having difficulties in school, Jim and his entire family went to a family counselor. Jim was very impressed with the work of the counselor. Considering the help and new direction his child and the whole family received, Jim developed a high regard for the counselor and thought that, "If I had done things differently, I could be doing that too, helping others *and* supporting my family."

More and more Jim thinks about what he's going to do with the rest of his life, but he doesn't talk about it too much for fear of disrupting what he knows is a good situation. With one child in college and another nearing graduation from high school, Jim wonders what he could possibly do for himself that wouldn't adversely affect his whole family. He knows he wants to do something different with his life—either move up in his present company or move in a different direction altogether. He also knows that it is important for him to continue to contribute to his family's stability and financial well-being.

Further, it is very important to him to maintain the respect he has earned in the community; he doesn't want to be seen as someone who has "gone off the deep end" in the much-talked-about mid-life crisis. Jim sees himself as a strong, independent, and caring person who just wants to feel more satisfied with his work. He knows that this "unsettled" nagging feeling is having a bad affect on him.

He wakes up one morning and decides to do something. If you were in Jim's shoes, what would you do?

At 38, Terry has quite a different story. By most people's standards, she is a successful artist. She has exhibited her work all over the state and last year had her first one-person showing in the city. She is basically pleased with her career.

But since her divorce from Bill last year, she finds herself having long periods of daydreaming and frequent bouts of insomnia. Even when things seem to be going well, Terry feels haunted by a sense of failure in her life.

She and Bill married early, both against their parents' wishes. Terry finished her freshman year the summer before they were married and helped support Bill through his last two years of college by taking assorted secretarial jobs, and giving evening art lessons in her small studio in their home. She remembers her parents' disappointment when she dropped out of college.

As she looks back, Terry wonders how she managed to find any time to paint for herself in those early years of her marriage. Of course, when Bill finished college and before their first child was born, Terry returned to college part-time and took several basic drawing and painting courses. She remembers those years as very happy and productive.

Although Terry and Bill have worked out a reasonable settlement regarding their children—the children spend at least two weekends a month and most school vacations with him—Terry is glad she works at her studio home to be available to her children as much as possible. The children are just at that age when they are very curious about their parents' earlier years and ask a lot of questions. "But, Mom, why didn't you finish college like Dad?" her daughter asks. "It doesn't seem fair. Even Grandma said it wasn't right . . ."

Terry has heard that before. Each time it makes her angry. True she loved her freshman year and loved the courses she took later. But she also loved Bill and was willing to help him through school—it seemed very important to them both at the time. She wishes she'd been able to return to college, too, "But it just wasn't to be." "Haven't I proven that success doesn't always require a college degree? Why does everyone keep reminding me that I haven't finished my 'education'? Maybe I have," she thinks. "And yet," she asks herself, "why does it make me so angry every time someone brings up the topic of completing a college degree?"

After months of this internal dialog with herself, Terry wakes up one morning and decides, "I'm going to do something about myself." If you were Terry, what would you do?

Both of these people *wanted* to do something to change their current situations or feelings about themselves. Before moving in any particular direction, as mature, responsible adults, they needed to look carefully at the complex, demanding situations in which they found themselves, consider their values and priorities and evaluate the resources—financial and otherwise—available to them. To do this, each sought out assistance from a variety of sources, some of which are described below:

- Through a recommendation made by the family counselor Jim highly respected, he contacted a career counselor who, over the course of several hour-long sessions, helped Jim determine that he really did want to pursue a new career in family counseling.

- Using several "inventories" and other self-evaluation tools, the counselor helped Jim identify his strengths, weaknesses, and priorities. The counselor then had Jim consider several *educational goals* to help him reach his life goal of becoming a family counselor. One thing was clear, however. Jim would need to get his 4-year college degree as quickly as possible to move on to graduate school.

- By reading several books recommended by the counselor, Jim learned that there was an "external degree" program in the State where he could apply to earn credits for college level knowledge he had obtained through his work and community activities, and that with some reading on his own, he could probably also earn credit through various credit by examination programs.

- Terry contacted the college she had originally attended and learned that it had a newly created "Returning Women's Program," to help women clarify their goals and map out new educational objectives.

- As a part of the program, Terry had access to a computerized-guidance program to allow her, at her own pace, to clarify her values, consider the merits of completing her degree in light of her success as an artist, and evaluate herself in a number of other ways.

- Terry met with an advisor on several occasions to discuss her sense of "failure" and her need to get back to feeling better about herself.

- Terry also began to meet other women like herself—women who wanted to bring significant change or resolution to their lives—and discovered that although her particular situation was unique, many of the feelings and self-doubts she had were not.

- After several months of talking with others and taking a hard look at what she wanted, Terry re-enrolled in her original college and began assembling a portfolio to earn credit in advanced art courses. She also enrolled in a correspondence program to complete her math and science requirements at home and began using the resources of her local library to help her brush up for a number of examinations for credit.

Jim and Terry are just two of thousands of adults who have enrolled in college in pursuit of new life goals. What they hadn't expected was the wide range of educational programs and services available to them to help them reach their educational objectives.

We hope that in conjunction with the information contained in this book you will seek out as much other information from your local colleges, libraries, career counseling centers, adult educational programs, state education departments, and even your employer, as you can. There are literally hundreds of educational tools and programs designed to fit your unique set of career and educational objectives.

Don't be afraid to explore!

Opportunities for Earning College Credit

Assessment of prior learning or "portfolio assessment" is but one means of demonstrating that you have acquired college-level knowledge on your own. Certainly there are many others that you will want to include in your "exploration." The checklist on page 17 will give you some idea of what these can include.

Credit by Examination

There are many credit-by-examination opportunities that offer 1½–3 hour examinations. These exams generally reflect college course work in specific subjects and are administered nationally several times a year at test centers located on college or university campuses.

Among the best known credit-by-examination programs are the College-Level Examination Program (CLEP), administered by Educational Testing Service, and the ACT-Proficiency Examination Program (ACT-PEP), administered by the American College Testing Company. Both of these provide a wide range of liberal arts, professional, and technical examinations.

Other credit-by-examination programs include Defense Activity for Non-Traditional Educational Support (DANTES), originally available only to military personnel and now available to the civilian population as well; the Advanced Placement Program (APP), a program intended primarily for high school students but whose examinations may be taken by anyone, regardless of age or background, and several others that are sponsored by colleges such as Ohio University, and Thomas A. Edison State College in New Jersey. Find out more about these programs by writing to the sponsoring agency at the addresses provided in Appendix A.

Other Opportunities

You may also want to explore television courses, courses offered by radio and newspapers, accredited correspondence programs, or the Program on Non-Sponsored Instruction (PONSI) through which several hundred corporate training programs and courses have been evaluated for credit by the American Council on Education (ACE) (see Appendix A). You may also have a professional license or certificate that can be recognized for college credit. It may take some investigating on your part, but it's well worth your time and effort to learn as much as you can about each of these credit-bearing opportunities. If you are already enrolled in college, find out about credit through departmental challenge examinations. All of these options go hand-in-hand with your portfolio planning.

Use this checklist to learn the ways you might earn college credit:

- ☐ Portfolio Assessment
- ☐ Credit-by-Examination
    - ☐ CLEP
    - ☐ ACT-PEP
    - ☐ DANTES
    - ☐ APP
    - ☐ College-sponsored credit-by-examination program
- ☐ Television, radio, and newspaper courses
- ☐ Evaluation of a license or certificate you now hold
- ☐ PONSI evaluation of training program you successfully completed
- ☐ College departmental challenge exams
- ☐ Courses taught in college classrooms, on campus, and in other off-campus locations
- ☐ Accredited college correspondence and independent study programs

---

What Does Assessment by Portfolio Involve?

Regardless of the other credit-earning methods you plan to explore, you bought this book because you want to learn about the most comprehensive way to earn the credit or advanced standing you deserve. The process of assessment by portfolio will help in this task. You may want to:

1. obtain college credits or the advanced standing you deserve to shorten the time required to earn a degree

Doug earned 15 credit hours for his knowledge of bookkeeping and accounting. He earned an additional six credits for his knowledge of personal finance and financial planning. Although Doug's work provided the basis for much of his learning, many people acquire knowledge of personal finance and financial planning from experiences not related to their work.

2. obtain permission to waive certain basic courses and take more advanced courses

3. meet professional requirements for licensure or certification

4. meet the requirements of an employer to obtain a promotion; and/or

5. satisfy yourself in knowing what college-level skills and competencies you actually have

Somewhere you undoubtedly heard that you *could* earn credit or advanced standing for your "life experience," "experiential learning," or "experiential knowledge." Although these words are sometimes used interchangeably, as you begin to think about yourself—your own background and experiences—you should focus on the words *knowledge* and *competence*. What *knowledge* and *skills* have you obtained from your work, your avocations, your reading? What learning experiences have you had that contributed to your *knowledge* or *skills* in journalism, drama, chemistry, business management, or whatever area you wish to consider?

This is a particularly important question because you will want to make sure that your self-expectations are reasonable. A common error is to assume that an experience in and of itself is worthy of college credit.

By way of example, Jean spent six months in France traveling with her husband who was overseas on business. During that time she took many fine photographs, learned to speak French fluently, and learned a good deal about French cooking and architecture.

Upon her return to the United States, very excited about her recent experiences, she enrolled at a college that offered an "assessment of prior learning" program. She went immediately to the assessment office seeking a year of college-credit for her "travel experience." She was, at first, terribly disappointed to learn that she was not eligible for a block of credits for what she felt had been the most enriching experience of her life. She was also troubled to learn that she would have to divide her experiences into several different segments and equate the segments with actual college courses offered at her institution. But after several discussions with her advisor and learning more about the assessment process, Jean decided to proceed with an assessment of her prior learning. Eventually she was awarded credit for her knowledge in photography, the French language, French culinary techniques, and the great cathedrals of France.

Obviously, Jean learned a great deal in her six months of traveling. However, the faculty assessors who evaluated her experiences needed to be sure that she had acquired *college-level knowledge* from her experiences—that is, *they expected her to have knowledge equivalent to that of students completing similar course work in their college classrooms*. It was up to Jean to *demonstrate* that she possessed the college-level knowledge she claimed to have.

So be sure, as you begin to consider the assessment process, that you focus on what it is you *know and can do,* not just on what you have experienced.

Focussing on defining what you know through the assessment process can have many lasting benefits beyond your immediate reasons for earning credit. It can provide you with a realistic appraisal of your learning which is important to you in planning further educational goals.

Assessment can also help you place the many dimensions of your learning into an integrated whole. Through assessment, you will develop fresh insight into your personal strengths as well as those areas in which you want to improve. This insight (and the confidence that results from it) can be valuable in work and academic settings.

Personally, the assessment process can help you build self-confidence, develop a sense of self-worth, and enable you to take risks in your life. A student in the Vermont State College system who successfully earned credits through the portfolio assessment process remarked: "I don't care how many credits I get. It (the assessment process) has changed my attitudes, my confidence in myself. I now know I can do things I was afraid to even try before."

Looking critically and carefully at the accomplishments of your life is a tremendous "psychological" boost. Students who begin by saying, "I haven't accomplished anything," often end by saying, "I didn't realize I had accomplished so much."

Summary

In this chapter, we discussed the importance of first identifying your life goals to help you develop clear educational objectives and in turn make maximal use of the many credit bearing opportunities available to you. We encouraged you to explore all the many programs and services available to you, keeping in mind that in all probability you will be able to find educational programs and services that will satisfy *your unique needs and circumstances.*

We urged you to focus on the *knowledge and skills* you have acquired, not just your experiences, as you begin to consider the assessment of your prior learning.

Lastly, we suggested that earning college credit for knowledge you already possess can have a lasting benefit, not the least of which is increasing your self confidence and self worth.

John earned an associate degree in automotive technology from his local community college. Because of his extensive knowledge and experience, John earned credit for his knowledge of basic automotive maintenance, engine diagnosis and tune-up, automotive engines and electricity, and automotive welding techniques. He also hopes to earn a bachelor's degree, since he now owns his own automotive repair business and anticipates earning credit for his knowledge of small business management—especially automotive management.

1.

The Preliminaries

Each believes naught but one's own experience.

—Empedocles

What You Need to Find Out

So now you are ready to begin. Right? Well, not quite. Before you actually begin the assessment process, you will want to make sure that any credits you earn will fit into your overall educational plan. To do this, you will want to get answers to the following questions:

1. Does your institution give credit or recognition for credits earned through portfolio assessment or the assessment of experiential learning?

2. If so, does the institution have a limit on the number of credits you can earn via this method? (At some institutions, separate limits are set on credits earned by each means—credit-by-examination, correspondence, PONSI, or portfolio. At others, they are lumped together. Make sure you find out your institution's policy *before* you begin.)

3. Can credits earned through your assessment apply to any aspect of your degree program or only to a selected portion, free electives, for example?
4. Will credits awarded for your prior learning be applied to your degree program immediately or only after particular course requirements have been met?
5. When should you begin the assessment process:
    - before you register at the college?
    - during the first semester?
    - after you have met certain requirements?
    - anytime?
6. What are the fees?
7. What printed materials, guidelines, and forms are you to use?
8. What personal assistance does the institution provide, such as workshops, advisors, or a course on assessment?
9. Is there a time restriction on the length of time in which you must complete your portfolio or assessment?
10. Who will assess your portfolio after it is developed?
    - college faculty
    - staff members from the assessment office
    - experts external to the institution
    - work supervisors
11. How and by whom are credit recommendations made?
12. Can you appeal a credit recommendation decision? If so, how?

Many of these questions may seem a bit overwhelming. More than likely, however, your institution will have a well-staffed Prior Learning Assessment Office, an Adult Learning Service Office, a Testing and Assessment Office, a Continuing Education Department, or an External Degree Program Office, with counselors or advisors eager to give you the answers you need. They may also have samples of other students' portfolios for you to review.

Don't be afraid to ask *any* other questions you think of, no matter how "silly" they may seem. Undertaking the assessment process requires a strong commitment of time, effort, and money. You will want to be sure that you know as clearly as possible what will be expected of you, so that you can put your best effort toward demonstrating that you really do possess the college-level knowledge you claim to have.

In the process of gathering all the information you need, you will also need to learn about the particular model of assessment used by your institution to turn your college-level knowledge into college credit. As is discussed in more detail in Chapter 4, there are three primary models currently in use:

1. The *College Course Model* requests that you equate your knowledge to specific college courses, using college catalog descriptions or course syllabi to guide you.

2. The *Learning Components Model* requires you to cluster your college-level skills and knowledge in a particular academic discipline, not limiting yourself to a particular college course description.

3. The *Block Credit Model* requires you to consider your college-level learning in light of the depth and breadth of knowledge obtained by someone who has graduated from college and who is employed in that particular field.

Consider all you will need to learn about your institution's policies and procedures if a portfolio development workshop or an assessment of prior learning course is offered, it would probably be in your best interest to take that course or workshop. By doing so, you will receive the most current, up-to-date information on your own institution's procedures and requirements, and you will have the opportunity to meet other interesting and motivated people who want to earn credit for what they already know.

At some institutions, you may even be able to earn college credit for taking the course! In short, it would probably be a good investment of your time, money, and energy.

Summary

In this chapter, we have emphasized the need to learn about your institution's policies and procedures before you begin the assessment process. By having as much knowledge as possible about these matters before you begin, you will be in a better position to work toward success!

1. The Preliminaries

Kim writes a weekly column for her local newspaper. She also works as a teacher's aide and is fluent in several foreign languages. She began her college program with six credit hours in journalism, six in teaching methods and 12 in foreign languages.

2.

Identifying Your College-Level Knowledge and Competence

Only so much do I know, as I have lived.

—Ralph Waldo Emerson

Reviewing Your Background and
Experience
Case Histories
The Dynamics of Learning
The Complexity of Knowledge and
Competence
Use of College Courses

Reviewing Your Background and Experience

Now, at last, you are truly ready to begin. At this stage of the process, you will identify the college-level knowledge and skills you possess that could be assessed through the portfolio or prior learning assessment process at your institution. To do this, you first need to look at as many relevant experiences as possible. Consider the following strategies:

1. Develop a chronological list of the jobs you have held, including part-time work.

2. Write a free-association list of people, places, and things from your past.

3. Conduct a "remember when" session with a family member, friend, or others who have known you over a significant length of time.

4. List key events, markers, or milestones in your life. Include successes and failures.

5. Develop an interest or hobby list. For each activity, write down the procedures you used and the products you developed.

6. Make a list of the books you have read over the last several years, concerts you have attended, museums you have visited.

7. Develop a list of non-credit courses you have taken or special training programs at your church or other community-based organization.

Or, you may wish to begin with a specific set of questions for yourself:

What Is My Job?
What do I have to know to do my job?

What have I learned that makes me good at my job?

What would I have to know (or say and do) to teach someone else my job?

What training programs have I attended?

What Special Skills Do I Have?
Have I given public presentations?

Have I assumed a leadership role in my church or synagogue?

Do I know CPR or first aid?

Do I speak a foreign language?

Can I draw, paint, play an instrument or dance?

Do I consider myself an expert in something not related to my job? Am I a mechanic, photographer, actor, church-school teacher, writer, etc.?

Have I done volunteer work in such areas as counseling, social services?

Do I have special skills in radio/tv, other audio-visual or technical competencies in any area?

Have I held an office or assumed a leadership role in a political party?

Have I developed or prepared public relations materials or other kinds of publicity for an organization?

How Do I Spend Leisure Time?
Do I have an absorbing interest in something which may be taught in college?

Do I read extensively in a particular field?

Do I go to museums or concerts on a regular basis?

Regardless of which strategy or which combination of strategies you use, you will want to make sure that the final list of your experiences is as thorough as possible, that for each one you can include dates and/or locations.

The first two columns on the sample Worksheet 1 (*page 38*) will help you organize your experiences. Whenever possible, group common or relevant experiences. This will help you in the next phase: identifying the learning that has occurred as a result of these experiences.

Once you feel that you have listed all the important experiences in your life, start to extract what you actually learned from these experiences. To do this, go down your list and ask yourself:

What do I do?

What did I have to know?

What did I learn?

The sample will help you complete your own worksheet. As you review Worksheet 1, note that different experiences can result in the same or similar learning. You will also see that a wide range of learning can transpire from a single experience.

WORKSHEET #1
Identifying What You Know

Year	Activity	What I Did	What I Had to Know	What I Learned
1977–1980	Held Administrative Assistant position, Union Community Service Agency	Maintained inventory control of publications	Organizational procedures	How to develop inventory control system
		Corresponded with clients	How to solve problems	How to write more effectively
		Wrote copy for press release	How to write business letters and memos	Public relations
		Prepared monthly budget reports	How to prepare news copy	How to deal with media representatives
		Supervised clerical staff	How to set up account books	How to monitor accounts receivable and accounts payable
			How to get along with others	Personnel policies and procedures
			How to deal with difficult personnel issues	Group dynamics
1978	Elected School Board Treasurer	Prepared budget proposals for Board's consideration	Thorough knowledge of State and local budget	Budgeting on a big scale
		Reviewed expenditures of school district	How to be careful	Fiscal management
		Worked with state auditors	How to explain budget and provide necessary information	Professional writing procedures
		Prepared budget statements for district newsletter	How to write	How to be persuasive
		Gave public presentations of Annual Budget Report	How to speak	How to improve my public speaking
				Public Relations

It is important to know that not all learning can be defined as college-level. As you consider the various aspects of your own life, extract those learning experiences that are college-level from those that are not. The following examples may help you to note this important distinction.

Case Histories

1. Laura, 28 years old, is married to an anthropologist. They have no children. From her hobby of ceramics she developed her own business, which has grown and currently employs 25 part-time workers. Laura also discovered that she had a writing talent, and has had several pieces of fiction published in children's magazines. She has read widely in American and English drama and goes to the theater frequently. She also spends a considerable amount of her leisure time walking in the parks in her community. She likes to talk with friends about what she has seen and thought about on her walks.

Before meeting her husband, Laura fell in and out of love several times and believes she has learned a lot about herself and human nature as a result of these experiences. She and her husband have traveled extensively in the United States and have visited a number of archaeological sites. She enjoys talking with her husband about the site visits and does extensive reading prior to each trip.

Laura has managed to accumulate 33 quarter-hours of college credit by taking courses part-time at the local community college. She now wishes to transfer this credit, receive recognition for her prior non-college experience, and work toward a baccalaureate degree with dual emphasis on business administration and ceramic production.

Possible Evaluation: Laura will probably have creditable knowledge and skill in the areas of ceramics, business management, prose writing, and American and English drama.

Although being in love is a highly significant human experience, what she has learned from this experience is highly subjective and not subject to verification by others. She likely will not receive credit or recognition toward her degree for these experiences.

Also, although her walks in the park have undoubtedly been very significant to her in thinking through her problems and enjoying the scenery, she will have a great deal of difficulty identifying knowledge and skills which have a conceptual base and/or are of college-level quality. She might be able to demonstrate her basic knowledge in the area of anthropology. She may receive recognition for knowledge in this area with a little additional reading to fill the gaps in her knowledge.

2. Jim is 48. Several years ago, he lost his wife and two children in an automobile accident in which he was charged with negligent driving. Coming through this experience, learning to live with his guilt by undergoing therapy, and adjusting to his new lifestyle made Jim feel that the experience has taught him quite a bit about himself and other people. He is presently the personnel manager of a local plant of a nationally recognized radio and television manufacturer.

He rose to his present position after 11 years in personnel administration with this company. For three of these 11 years, he lived and worked in Brazil. In preparation for this job, he used Spanish and Portuguese records to learn to speak the languages. While in Brazil, he traveled extensively through South America and learned a lot about cultural differences. He has written three articles for a professional journal in the field of personnel management.

For 20 years, Jim has had an interest in modern architecture. He has traveled extensively in the United States, visiting well-known examples of modern architecture. He has read widely in the field. He has served as a lay leader and board member in his local church. He has read pertinent church literature and participated in an adult study group over a six-year period.

Jim would now like to go to college and pursue a liberal arts degree.

He feels he should receive substantial credit for the experiences that he has obtained outside of a formal learning setting.

Possible Evaluation: Jim will most likely receive appropriate recognition or credit in the areas of personnel management, foreign language, and professional writing. In order to receive

Pat now works as a policewoman. She earned 24 credit hours for her knowledge and training in criminal justice. Prior to joining the police force, Pat held a position in the U.S. military and later, as a civilian, worked for her city government in public safety. Altogether, Pat earned 52 credit hours for her prior learning.

credit for his knowledge of modern architecture, Jim will need to have it evaluated by an expert in the field. This may be done in several ways. The expert might interview Jim, evaluate an essay on modern architecture Jim had written, or both. If, in the opinion of the expert, Jim's knowledge has sufficient breadth and depth to qualify as college-level learning, the evaluator will make an appropriate recommendation for credit.

If Jim can demonstrate that the leadership and management skills that he developed as a result of his experience in his local church are generally applicable to other situations and do not duplicate skills developed on his job, he could receive some additional credit.

Although the loss of his family was undoubtedly significant and traumatic, Jim will probably not be able to convey to others the insights that he gained about himself and other people through this experience. It would be difficult, if not impossible, to demonstrate the applicability of the knowledge gained through his experience to other situations or settings.

3. Carmen was born in Puerto Rico 47 years ago. Along with several other members of her family, she owns a small high-fashion dress shop. People are often surprised to hear Carmen's story. Carmen's earliest recollections are of her mother and grandmother sewing. To supplement the family income, the women took in mending and also made most of the family's clothing. Carmen remembers helping with the sewing from the time she was old enough to hold a needle. She still recalls with a smile the wedding dress she had designed and sewn for her cousin just before leaving Puerto Rico for New York City.

Coming to New York after high school in hopes of finding a "real" job, Carmen lived with her brother and sister-in-law and began working at the same clothing manufacturing company as her sister-in-law. Working in a large factory, Carmen learned to operate the powerful industrial sewing machines and so much more! She learned the language and customs of English-speaking Americans and enjoyed telling about the life and customs of Puerto Rico. She also took courses in English which were designed for people whose first languages were other than English. From there she took several other courses in local adult schools, mostly in the areas of fashion and design.

After marrying her husband and beginning her family, Carmen, like her mother and grandmother, began taking in sewing to supplement the family income. She had never stopped making her own clothes and often those of close friends and family members when she wanted to give a special gift.

With so many outside dressmaking requests coming in, Carmen quit her regular job and with her family's support—emotional as well as financial—opened a small store devoted to designing, producing and selling exclusive women's clothes, "Carmen's Fashions." In spite of the early struggles, after almost ten years the business has become very successful.

While Carmen considers herself very fortunate to have accomplished so much in what she refers to as "her New York life," she still feels strong ties with her family and the life of Puerto Rico. She regularly reads newspapers from Puerto Rico and returns as often as she can to visit. She believes that earning a college degree, while not necessary for the success of her business, would give her a deep sense of personal satisfaction. She would like to earn credit for as much of her prior learning as possible.

Possible Evaluation: No doubt Carmen will be able to earn credit for her native Spanish. She probably will also be able to earn credit for her knowledge and skill in clothing construction and design, fashion merchandising and retailing, as well as small business management. In addition, she may be able to earn credit for her knowledge of the history and culture of Puerto Rico.

4. Sharon is 43. At the age of 18 she entered the local community college and pursued a general liberal arts program with no clear career objective. She received her AA degree at 20 and married. Since then, she has been a homemaker for herself, two children (ages 17 and 15), and a husband. Throughout her child-raising years, she read numerous books and articles and discussed them with her pediatrician. The pediatrician had recommended much of Sharon's reading.

Sharon has also read extensively in the consumer economics field and applied much of her reading in decorating her home. She is a skilled, award-winning clothing designer. She enjoys gourmet cooking. Her husband frequently comments on how much he values her companionship and support. He says that he could not have achieved the success in his career that he currently enjoys without her help.

Sharon participates in a number of civic organizations. She was president of the PTA and vice president of the local chapter of the League of Women Voters. In her spare time, she enjoys playing tennis.

Sharon's children are growing up and she finds herself less content with homemaking. She is not sure what career, if any, she would like to pursue. She feels enrolling for a B. A. degree program will help her find an area of interest. She hopes her years of experience will count toward the degree.

Possible Evaluation: Although raising two children has been an important part of Sharon's life, she should not expect college credit for that activity alone. However, since she has attempted to conceptualize the rearing of children through reading and discussion, she may be able to demonstrate creditable knowledge at the college level in the areas of general psychology and child development. Also, she might receive credit in the fields of home economics, organizational leadership, and tennis.

5. Ted is 45, married, and has three children. He has worked for seven years as a licensed real estate salesman. He also worked his way through a self-instructional textbook in salesmanship. He has participated in three on-the-job training workshops totaling 60 contact hours.

Ted is a member of Toastmasters International and has given a number of speeches to service clubs. He is president of the local chapter of the Junior Chamber of Commerce and has served as president of the local chapter of the Lions Club. He also serves as an elected member of the City Council.

For nine years, Ted has read widely in photography during his leisure time. He presently owns $2,500 worth of basic equipment. He has won several awards at amateur photography showings and he has had two "one-man" shows in his community. Over the past six years, he has had considerable experience in backpacking and camping, and has read countless books and articles on the subjects. Two years ago he took a course in survival training. Once, he and two other men survived one week in a wooded, mountainous area living "off the land." He has many friends in his home community and is considered to be an excellent host when entertaining at home.

Ted now wants to move up into a management position within his present real estate firm. Company policy requires that he have at least an Associate Degree in order to hold a management position. Ted wants to enter the local community college to pursue a degree, and feels that his past experience should count toward his degree.

Possible Evaluation: Ted might be able to receive college credit in the area of real estate appraisal, sales, photography, and public speaking. His knowledge of backpacking and camping might be recognized as being comparable to a Physical Education course required by some colleges. His child development knowledge is probably not at a college level. His skill as a good host is probably not applicable to a college course credit.

6. June is 32 and single. She took a secretarial program in a business college immediately upon graduation from high school. She worked as a secretary for five years and then moved to office supervisor for three years. She had a drinking problem which began in high school and became increasingly severe during the time that she worked as a secretary.

The pressures of serving as an office supervisor greatly contributed to her drinking until the consumption of alcohol began to adversely affect her job performance. Finally, she took the advice of her doctor and was briefly hospitalized. She joined Alcoholics Anonymous and has not had an alcoholic drink since. She feels that she learned a considerable amount about herself and human behavior as a result of her bout with alcoholism. Following her hospitalization, June resumed working as a secretary and also has worked for the past five years as a volunteer aide in the psychiatric ward of a general hospital. She has taken in-service courses and has worked closely with a psychiatric social worker.

Over the last four years, June has served as a volunteer in the hospital's annual fund drive, and rose from "worker" to "team captain" in the drive. She helped to write a procedural manual for conducting the fund drive and has read several standard textbooks and numerous articles and pamphlets on the general subject of abnormal psychology.

June now wants to go to graduate school in psychology. In order to be admitted to graduate school, she needs a baccalaureate degree. June feels that her experience should earn her credit to be applied toward a degree.

Possible Evaluation: June may receive creditable recognition for the subjects of abnormal psychology, secretarial science, office supervision, and fund raising. Her experience in helping to write a procedural manual is likely to be too narrow to be applicable toward a college credit. Although her success in overcoming alcoholism probably will not lead directly to college credit, certainly her experience as a counselor and volunteer, particularly if she had read a good deal in these areas, might.

7. Bill is 29 and single. Immediately upon graduation from high school he joined the Air Force. While in the service, he assisted in running a post exchange and feels he learned a considerable amount about bookkeeping and inventory control. He was stationed in Germany for two years.

Seven years ago, Bill founded a small gift shop that he now operates. He feels he has learned advertising and merchandising through his experience and through reading and taking noncredit seminars. He has traveled extensively in Europe in order to purchase merchandise for his store and knows French and German well enough to transact business in these languages.

He feels he has learned quite a bit about cultural differences and some of the history of Europe. He has also become an accomplished gourmet cook. Bill now wishes to pursue a Bachelor of Business Administration Degree at a local state university. He feels that his experiences should be recognized in meeting the requirements for his degree.

Possible Evaluation: Bill could receive credit for the subject areas of French and German, accounting, inventory control, and small business management. His knowledge of cultural differences and history will probably not be equivalent to college level work, and he will not receive college credit unless his learning is supplemented by further study. It is possible he will receive credit for his skill in gourmet cooking.

8. Erik is 39 years old. At 16 he dropped out of high school, much against his mother's wishes. Erik's father had died suddenly when Erik was 11. At 16, Erik felt angry and troubled and could see no reason to finish high school. He thought it would be much better to work and contribute to his family's very limited income.

For almost four years, Erik changed jobs every few months—from dishwasher, to gas station attendant, to carpenter's assistant, or "go-fer" as Erik would call it now. Nothing seemed to hold his interest and he never seemed to have enough money for the things he wanted: a car that didn't break down, new clothes, a ring for his girlfriend.

Quite by chance, Erik learned that a local automotive plant would be hiring assemblers and much to his surprise, Erik was among those hired. Although the hours were long, for the first time in his life, Erik's wages seemed fair, he had health insurance and other benefits, and more than that, he liked the idea of contributing to a quality product. He also liked the idea of belonging to the union. Erik was well liked by his fellow workers, and his supervisors were often complimentary.

About the time he and his young wife were expecting their first child, Erik was offered an opportunity to participate in a special training program in diesel engine technology which would provide him with an opportunity to learn new skills and eventually to earn more money. He grabbed the opportunity.

Over the years, Erik has continued to move up in his company, and has become increasingly involved in his union. Along the way, he passed the GED (General Educational Development tests) so he now has the equivalency of a high school diploma.

Most recently Erik was offered an opportunity to participate in a training program for supervisors. Although he has eagerly taken advantage of this opportunity, he knows that to continue in this direction, sooner or later he may need a college degree. He woud like to earn college credit for his prior learning to speed up the process.

Possible Evaluation: However much he may have learned about life, Erik's early experiences probably did not provide him with a thorough enough knowledge of or skills in any single field to earn college credit. Because of the extensiveness of the training program and his work experience, Erik may be able to earn credit in principles of diesel engines, diesel brake systems, transmissions and clutches, hydraulics, and diesel welding. He may also be able to earn credit for this knowledge of unions and negotiation.

How would you write your own story?

The Dynamics of Learning

Consider the following examples and reflect on your own learning experiences. Keep in mind that learning can proceed from the most general to more specific, or from the most specific to the more general.

Starting Point

All through high school I
had a general interest in American History;
Later, my interest about Twentieth Century America increased;
I focused my reading on the Twenties, The Jazz Age;
A few years ago, I began reading extensively about
the Cold War Since World War II;
I have followed American Foreign Policy very closely
since the Vietnam War

In this case, a general interest led to greater specificity in knowledge, reflecting greater in-depth knowledge of a particular field. We learn many things this way. Think back to science, math, or literature courses you may have had in elementary or high school. Remember those "introduction to" courses that were prerequisites to the in-depth courses that looked *really* interesting? Undoubtedly, as you consider your background, you will find that much of your learning has developed in this pattern.

It may well be, however, that you have learned a lot going from the very specific to the more general. Look at the next example. Aren't there things you've learned in this way, too?

Starting Point

1975 studied typing in high school
1977 learned stenography at adult education program

2. Identifying

1978 held steno-typist position
1980 assumed administrative duties
1980–82 learned basic accounting and read several
books on financial and personnel management
1983 took certificate program in management
1984 appointed office manager

Many work experiences follow this pattern, so be sure to look at all of the steps that have led to your current position, interest, or level of expertise.

The Complexity of Knowledge and Competence

In general, the credit you receive through the assessment of prior learning is directly related to the *complexity* of your knowledge, regardless of *how* you learned a particular subject. From simple facts and names at your first level of knowledge, you may have progressed to more complicated skills like analysis, comparison, and evaluation. This may help you to describe your learning using the following guidelines:[1]

How Do You Define the Specifics of your Learning?

- Do you know the *terminology* of the field?
- Do you know *specific facts?*
- Do you have knowledge of *conventions?*
- Do you have knowledge of *trends and sequences?*
- Do you have knowledge of *classifications and categories?*
- Do you have knowledge of *criteria?*
- Do you have knowledge of *methodology?*
- Do you have knowledge of *principles and generalizations?*
- Do you have knowledge of *theories and structure?*

Verbs that help you answer these questions:

I know
I can

relate	record
list	define
repeat	recall
name	

I have memorized

---

[1] Adapted from Bloom's Taxonomy of Educational Objectives

How Do You Convey What You Know?

- Can you *translate* what you know?
- Can you *interpret* what you know?
- Can you *extrapolate* from what you know?

Verbs: I can

restate	identify
discuss	locate
describe	report
recognize	review
explain	tell
express	

How Can You Apply Your Knowledge?

Verbs: I can

demonstrate	schedule
operate	sketch
apply	employ
use	practice
illustrate	

How Can You Analyze Your Knowledge?

- Can you analyze *elements* of the subject field?
- Can you analyze *relationships* in the field?
- Can you analyze *organizational* principles?

Verbs: I can

distinguish	differentiate	diagram
analyze	appraise	inspect
calculate	test	debate
relate	compare	inventory
experiment	contrast	question
criticize	solve	examine

How Can You Synthesize What You Know?

- Can you *produce* a unique communication about this field?
- Can you *develop* a plan or a proposed set of operations?
- Can you *derive* a set of abstract relations?

Verbs: I can

compose	assemble	organize
plan	collect	manage
propose	construct	prepare
design	create	formulate
arrange	set up	

Can You Evaluate What You Know?

- Can you make judgments based on *internal evidence?*
- Can you make judgments based on *external evidence?*

Verbs: I can   **judge**   **appraise**
              score   **select**
              evaluate   **choose**
              rate   **assess**
              compare   **estimate**
              value   **measure**
              revise

Not all of these questions and verbs will apply to what you know. But by using what seems to apply to your own field of knowledge and experience, you will be well on your way to identifying what it is you really do know.

Use of College Courses

Another resource available to you for identifying what you know is course descriptions which are found in college catalogs.* Many descriptions of what will be covered in a course also indicate the *level* of expertise expected. Look at several different catalog descriptions. While course titles from one institution to another may appear to be similar, what is covered may be quite different. Since you want to be able to identify in your portfolio exactly what it is *you* know, one description may be more helpful to you than another. Look at these three different sample descriptions for business communications courses:

English 127—Basic Business English: *3 credits/*
The student will learn the fundamentals of business and office communications through a review of the mechanics of the English language and the basic types of business communication.

English 420—Business Writing: *3 credits/*
Application of business writing to the preparation of common letter types, reports, and advertising copy. Sales, adjustment collection and employment letters are stressed.

Business 315/Business Report Writing: *3 credits/*
Emphasis on communication theory as applied to the analysis

---

* For a full description of college catalogs and information on how to receive them, see "An Adult Guide to Understanding Colleges" in Chapter 6.

and preparation of information and analytical reports. Covers the use of formal and informal reports in a wide variety of organizational settings.

As you will see, each of these descriptions is very different. English 127 covers fundamental writing skills necessary in business situations. English 420 is a higher level course because it includes reports, advertising copy, and very specific letter styles. Business 315 is the most advanced of the three courses because it stresses theory, analysis, and formal report preparation.

Identify which single course description fits your knowledge best or which of the combined skills and competencies best reflects your knowledge.

You may also find that reading the many varied college catalog descriptions will put your learning into a new perspective. You may be surprised at some of the courses that will help you to define what you know and can earn college credit for.

Look at the following examples:

The American Musical: *3 credits/*
A survey of the development of the American musical from minstrel shows to the present. Exploration of America's most unique contribution to world theatre in its various manifestations, on and off Broadway, in films, on showboats, and in cabarets. Films and field trips provide broader exposure to this theatre form.

Safety and First Aid: *3 credits/*
The course content includes American Red Cross certification in Standard First Aid and Personal Safety and Multimedia Standard First Aid. The opportunity to qualify for an instructor's rating for Standard First Aid is available to persons showing outstanding performance and knowledge of content. Safety education as it relates to schools and the community prepares one to provide a leadership role as a teacher, parent, and as a member of society.

Auto Mechanics: *3 credits/*
Laboratory experiences are provided with automobile engine analysis, adjustment, repair and overhaul and chassis running-gear adjustment and repair. Emphasis is placed on practical work with a range of different types of engines and automobiles.

Floral Design I: *3 credits/*
Basic principles of design as applied to floral arranging. Emphasis is placed on the primary types of arrangements including centerpiece, vase, corsage, tray, and mantel. A commercial production rate is stressed.

Murder Will Out: The Mystery Story: *3 credits/*
Extensive readings in the major authors of mystery/detective fiction from Poe to the present to illustrate the history, nature, variety, psychology, and morality of this popular genre. Reading includes criticism. Emphasis on great and classic puzzlers.

General Electricity: *3 credits/*
Studies basic principles of electricity, laws, theories, devices, instruments and testing equipment. Emphasizes direct and alternating current circuits and devices. An examination of electron theory, resistance, inductance, and capacitance allows the student to analyze and generalize as to the behavior and characteristics of electric current. Laboratory experiences allow students to experiment and apply their learnings to problem solving situations.

The Bible as Literature: *4 credits/*
Intensive reading of Genesis, Exodus, Ecclesiastes, and Job with special reference to how these stories have recurred in Western literature.

Basic Nutrition: *3 credits/*
Studies human nutrition for basic knowledge of nutrients and psychological processses in the utilization of food and for some understanding of the ways in which age, health, social and economic factors and other variables affect nutritional needs and food practices.

Water Safety Instructor: *3 credits/*
The Water Safety Instructor course is comprised of the American National Red Cross standardized program of skill proficiency, teaching methodologies, principles of class organization, safety factors in teaching swimming, and practice teaching experiences. The course is for advanced swimmers who are interested in learning to teach swimming and water safety. Prerequisites for candidates in the Water Safety Instruction Course include a minimum age of 17 and the possession of a current American National Red Cross Advanced Life Saving Certificate as well as the ability to perform swimmer skills. Upon successful completion of this course, the student will receive the American National Red Cross Certificate as a Water Safety Instructor.

Keypunch Operator: *2 credits/*
Knowledge and skill in keypunch operation. Students completing this course will have sufficient capability in keypunch operation for initial employment.

Basic Drawing: *3 credits/*
Examines the fundamentals of seeing line and value through studies of nature, still life arrangements, the human figure, and concepts of perspective. Various media are used including ink, charcoal, and graphite.

Campaigns and Corruption: *4 credits/*
An examination of post-1960 innovations and trends in political party recruitment. Techniques and management of political campaigns are stressed, and opportunity for field experience at the state and local level provided.

Welding Processes I: *3 credits/*
A study of Gas Welding (OGW) and Shielded Metal Arc Welding (SMAW) processes with industrial applications. The theory behind the proper procedure of gas welding, cutting, and brazing are developed. Welding laboratory projects supplement the lecture material.

English as a Foreign Language: *Variable Credit/*
Use of the present tenses in obtaining and giving information and in describing. Basic sentence patterns, intonation and pronunciation. Vocabulary development up to 3,000 words (active acquisition) and 6,000 words (passive acquisition).

Basic Electronics: *3 credits/*
Provides the fundamental subject material in current flow and direct current circuits.

Weaving: *3 credits/*
Study of weaving, its materials, techniques and concepts as a means of artistic expression. Exploration of effective methods of communication through weaving by a variety of assignments. Various steps in the weaving process: spinning fibers, tapestry techniques, and plain weave.

Fire Fighting Tactics and Strategy: *3 credits/*
Efficient and effective utilization of manpower, equipment, and apparatus. Emphasis on pre-planning, fire ground organization, problem solving related to fire ground decision making, and attack tactics and strategy.

Contemporary Black Literature: *3 credits/*
Recent literature by Black Americans in relation to literary trends and values as well as prevailing social conditions.

Here, Mike, who works for a major automotive company, is adjusting the hydraulic pressure on the cylinder block face finishing machine. Mike was able to earn nine credit hours for the company-sponsored training program he participated in and an additional six credit hours for his special knowledge of electronics. Mike is making extensive use of his company's tuition-assistance program to help him pay for his college education.

College Credit for What You Know

Plastics Technology: *2 credits/*
A comprehensive overview that includes the definition and history of plastics, types of plastics, simple chemistry of plastics, assembly techniques in thermo plastics: automotive, aircraft, business machines, appliance field and industrial applications.

Human Sexuality and Family Life: *3 credits/*
A course designed to explore healthy family life with four major areas of concentration: interpersonal relationships, foundations of human growth development, responsible personal behavior, and establishment of strong family life. Particular emphasis is given to the implication each area of concentration has on the health of the individual, family and community.

Each of the preceding courses reflects knowledge often gained by independent learning through adult education courses, independent reading, community involvement, military training, or simply many years of solving practical problems or pursuing long-standing interests. As you consider your background, be sure to look at *all* you know and can do. Don't underestimate the importance of what you've done and learned in all facets of your life!

Further Use of Course Descriptions

In some assessment of prior learning or portfolio assessment programs you will be expected to provide actual course descriptions as a means of identifying your knowledge. The credit recommendations made by your portfolio "assessors" will be based on those *particular* course descriptions. In this case, you will want to be especially careful to pick the ones most appropriate for you. Look, for example, at the next three "Introduction to Psychology" course descriptions.

PSY 105; Introduction to Psychology: *3 credits/*
The student will demonstrate an understanding of psychology as a science, and how it works for and against him in his everyday life. The student will cover the important topics of sensation and perception, learning, and psychological tests and measurements. Emphasis will be on developing a clear idea of the nature of psychology and its investigations.

PSY 200; Introduction to Psychology: *3 credits/*
General characteristics of human behavior, including motivation, learning, development, thinking, perception, sensation

and measurement. The objectives are: development of the ability to communicate in written and oral form accurately and scientifically about behavior; development of an understanding of and a capacity to use scientific ideas and processes as they apply to behavior, an understanding of the behavior of organisms.

PSY 101; Introduction to Psychology: *3 credits/*
An introduction to the general principles that influence behavior. Topical discussion is arranged into three modules: module one involves history of psychology, research methods, learning and retention; module two describes the nervous system, sensation, perception, development, maturation, and heredity; module three consists of personality theory, the study of groups and attitude formation.

In all three cases, the course titles and number of credits awarded are the same. However, a close inspection reveals several differences. Whereas Psych. 105 emphasizes the impact of psychology on the student and its place in the world of science, Psych. 200 emphasizes the development of the ability to communicate using psychological language. Psych. 101 focuses on the history of psychology, aspects of human behavior, and more detailed areas of the study of psychology.

This difference also occurs in various business fields. Look at the next examples for courses in accounting.

ACC 202; Cost Accounting: *3 credits/*
Prerequisite: Principles of Accounting II/
Instruction in the principles of cost accounting and the keeping of cost records. Involves a detailed study of job order, process, and standard costs systems and a survey of other costing techniques and applications.

ACC 03:010:451; Cost Accounting: *3 credits/*
Prerequisites; ACC 03:010:274, Managerial Accounting/
Open only to accounting majors or by special permission.

Basic cost concepts and the operation of two basic cost systems (job order and process costs), including problems involving multiple product costing and standard cost with emphasis in variance analysis.

As with the psychology courses, the course titles and number of credits awarded are exactly the same. Again though, a closer inspection reveals significant differences.

Whereas ACC 202 requires Principles of Accounting II as a prerequisite, ACC 03:010:451 requires Managerial Accounting, which in turn, when you look it up in the catalog, requires Financial Accounting as a prerequisite. So, to document your knowledge in cost accounting using the course description for ACC: 03:010:451, you would probably need to demonstrate knowledge of Managerial Accounting and Financial Accounting. This is fine if you have that knowledge—there are so many more credit bearing opportunities for you—but if not, you may want to look for a course description more like the one for ACC 202.

The same also applies in technical fields. Check out the examples given in fluid mechanics.

23ME256 Fluid Mechanics: *3 credits/*
Prerequisite: 23ME233 Thermodynamics I./
Kinematics and dynamics of fluid flow. Hydrostatic forces: rotational and irrotational flow, stream and velocity potential functions, two-dimensional planar flow; Euler's and Bernoulli's dynamical equations for fluid motion; application of impulse momentum equations; hydraulic machinery; fluid viscosity in laminar and turbulent flow; dimensional analysis and dynamical similarity of models; frictional energy losses of flow systems; dynamics of lift and drag.

PHY221: Fluid Mechanics: *3 credits/*
Prerequisites: MAT 111, PHY 115. Lec 3 hrs./
The properties and behavior of fluids: density, pressure, fluid statics, buoyancy, hydraulic devices. Course examines fluid dynamics, continuity of flow. Bernoulli's equation, Benturi's principle, the Pitot tube, and fundamentals of dynamic lift orifices, nozzles, tubes, valves, and other applications of flow-control devices. Discussions of viscosity and flow losses are incorporated.

As in the cost accounting example, the course titles and the number of credits awarded are exactly the same but a closer inspection reveals significant differences. 23ME256: Fluid Mechanics, taken from one college catalog, lists Thermodynamics as a prerequisite. When you look up Thermodynamics in the same catalog, you find that it has two prerequisites, General Chemistry and Differential Equations. Each of these courses, in turn, has prerequisites. Therefore, to document your knowledge for credit in 23ME256 you may be expected to demon-

2. Identifying

strate knowledge of nine different prerequisite courses! If, in fact, you possess that knowledge, then there are that many more credit-bearing opportunities for you. But if not, you may want to look for a course description better suited to your needs.

PHY221: Fluid Mechanics, from a second college catalog, reflects a less theoretical approach to the field. It has two prerequisites, applied college mathematic and mechanics, neither with additional prerequisites.

To do this, plan to examine at least three catalogs (one each from a two-year school, a four-year college, and a university). You can find catalogs in your local public library or in a nearby college.

The school from which you are seeking credit may, however, require you to use its own course descriptions. In this case, look carefully at the range of courses offered in your area of expertise and pick the ones that most closely parallel your knowledge and skills.

Summary

In this chapter we have looked at techniques and resources you can use to identify what it is you know. We have suggested that you

1. Compile a list of your experiences, activities, accomplishments, books you've read, etc.

2. Consider *how* you've gained the knowledge you possess from either a general base to more in-depth specificity or from a specific skill to a broader base.

3. Identify the specifics of what you know by considering six different facets of learning: KNOWLEDGE, COMPREHENSION, APPLICATION, ANALYSIS, SYNTHESIS and EVALUATION.

4. Use college catalogs to help you identify not only what you know but what will be *expected* of you in your assessment.

5. Use college course descriptions to help you describe and define your learning.

In the next chapter, we will discuss how you can document the college-level learning that you have identified in this chapter.

Bill is a personnel officer in a large corporation. He earned 21 credit hours for his knowledge of personnel management and business communications. In addition to his job, Bill also serves as a volunteer at a recreation center in his community. From his experience and supplemental reading, he was able to earn an additional nine credits for his knowledge of group dynamics, recreation leadership and recreation program planning.

Documenting What You Know and Can Do

No person's knowledge can be beyond his (or her) experience.

—John Locke

Documenting Resources
Documenting Steps
Documentation Supplements
The Problem of Knowledge of
Competence But No Documentation

In order for you to receive college credit for what you know and can do, you must provide evidence, or documentation of your learning. This can take many forms: a computer program you've written, a tape of a piano recital you gave, a letter from an employer outlining your job responsibilities and describing your performance. Just as students in a classroom must provide evidence of their learning in the form of book reports, oral presentations, research papers or examination results, so too, you will be expected to demonstrate that you really do possess the

61

knowledge you claim to have. In this chapter we will look at different kinds of documentation you may be able to use and how best to obtain that documentation.

Documentation Resources

No doubt when you were completing Worksheet 1 in Chapter II or compiling lists of your experiences or activities, you recalled specific people, projects, or reports that were critical to your success. These could serve as your documentation resources.

Documentation resources usually fall into two categories: direct and indirect. Direct documentation refers to products you have produced, performances you have given, reports you have written, marketing plans you have produced, etc. In most cases, direct documentation serves as the strongest evidence that you really do know what you claim to.

Examples of direct evidence include:

- Photographs you have taken
- Poems, plays, stories, or articles you have written
- Audio or audio/visual tapes of performances you have given
- Music you have composed
- Musical scores you have arranged
- Computer programs you have written
- Dresses you have designed and sewn
- Manuals or brochures you have written or designed
- Patents you have obtained
- Architectural drawings you have done
- Paintings, sculptures, or drawings you have created
- Curriculum plans you have prepared

Indirect documentation is usually information *about* you and your accomplishments. It can take the form of:

- Letters written on your behalf by
  Employers
  Co-workers
  Business partners
  Business consultants
  Teachers
  Church, community, or government leaders
  Professional association members

- Commendations you may have received
- Program notes from peformances you have given or exhibits in which you have shown your work
- Magazine or newspaper articles about you and your accomplishments

Weak sources of documentation, which should be avoided, include:

- Letters from
  Family members
  Your own students or clients
  Your own employees
  Friends who might serve as "personal references" in other contexts
- Travel brochures of places you have visited

Regardless of what documentation you have available or select to use, remember that their chief purpose is to *verify* that you have the college level knowledge you claim to have. Think very carefully about which pieces of documentation you have or can get that best reflect your college-level learning. Below, we have outlined several documentation steps that may be helpful to you.

Documentation Steps

1. *Identify What You Know.* You can only begin to think about documenting your knowledge *after* it's identified. Before requesting or assembling your documentation, be sure you know what learning it is you're trying to verify. If necessary, review the suggestions in Chapter II for identifying your college-level knowledge.

2. *List Your Documentation Resources.*
   A. For direct documentation, inventory the pieces you plan to use. Do you know where they are? Is your best painting on the wall in your local library or in your studio? Is a co-worker using your curriculum plan at the kindergarten or is a copy in your study? After you prepare your inventory, organize all the pieces you plan to use in one location.

   B. For indirect documentation, make a list of all the people who could potentially serve to document your knowledge and abilities. Be as thorough as possible. If you operated a small business, you might initially think only of your partner. But what about your attorney, your tax accountant, or your banker? Often two or three letters (from different sources) that *verify* the same aspect of your knowledge prove complementary to each other. One writer may emphasize in a paragraph what another glosses over in a sentence.

Gather articles you have about yourself, program notes listing you as a participant in the performances, or commendations you may have received for outstanding work in a volunteer organization. Add these to your resources materials. They'll come in very handy.

3. *Request the Documentation You Need.* This process may take time, so begin to gather your direct documentation much earlier than you definitely need it. If you have paintings, displays, or other pieces of your work out on display or loan, call or write to make arrangements to retrieve them. You may not want or be able to retrieve a large painting or mural. In this case, make arrangements to have high-quality photographs or slides made of your work. In the case of written materials, make sure to have duplicate copies made to include in your portfolio.

To obtain the necessary indirect documentation, begin by contacting each person twice—once by phone or in person, and again in writing. Explain why you want the documentation, mention the assessment program and the college or university by name, and discuss how the documentation will help you.

Specify exactly what knowledge you want documented because only documentation that VERIFIES learning can be used to document what you know. Make sure that the letter written on your behalf is not simply a letter of recommendation. (Note the distinction provided in the following examples.)

When you decide who you would like to have write on your behalf, be sure to choose those who have had the opportunity to observe your work directly. Make sure that the directness of your relationship with this individual comes across in the letter. (Sample letter "C" may help you request the information you need.)

3. Documenting

Sample Letter A

This is essentially a letter of recommendation. It would be inappropriate to serve as a letter of validation in your portfolio:

Dear Assessment Office:

I am writing this letter on behalf of Nancy A. Rotolo, who worked for the Town of East Overthere as an auditor for the last three years. I have been Town Manager for the last six years. Ms. Rotolo reported directly to me during the three years she worked for the Town.

Ms. Rotolo performed her work as an auditor in a timely and thorough manner. She was prompt in completing assignments. She was willing to take on added assignments when necessary. One example of this was financial work that she readily assumed for the local elementary school.

I am certain that Ms. Rotolo will succeed in whatever work she attempts. If she were available, we would certainly consider her for rehire.

Sincerely,

Thomas Chen

Sample Letter B

This is a good example of a letter of validation.

Mr. Donald Lyons
Diamond College
Assessment office
456 Espirit Street
Newtown, MI 04371

Dear Mr. Lyons:

I am writing to you in response to a request I received from Mrs. Barbara Ackerman. She has requested me to provide evidence of her accounting skills in connection with an assessment of prior learning to be done by your institution. I worked with

Barbara several years ago when I was performing an audit of the Town of Hillsboro. At that time I was an Audit Manager with the firm of Gordon & Sherman in Hillsboro and I was responsible for all field work.

Barbara, at the time, was the accountant for the Town of Hillsboro. In that capacity she performed essentially the entire accounting function for the town. As I recall, her responsibilities included:

1. Complete responsibility for maintaining the records of the town on the computer based (IBM System 32) system used by the town.

2. She, in fact, performed most of the work in connection with a conversion from a manual accounting system to the computer based system. This included solving significant problems which arose in connection with the conversion of records formerly maintained on an unsatisfactory magnetic card electronic data processing, bookkeeping machine to the IBM system.

3. Barbara had a good working knowledge of the various concepts of municipal accounting.

4. Barbara was responsible for coordination of the audit performed by my firm. She prepared all of the accounting schedules that were needed in the performance of the audit. This included bank reconciliations of all bank accounts and various other schedules requested.

In summary, it was obvious to me that Barbara Ackerman was performing all of the responsibilities of her position as town accountant exceptionally well. She was extremely competent in that position and in my opinion the town lost a valuable asset when Barbara left.

I believe Barbara has demonstrated skills in the accounting area which are far beyond those expected of someone with her level of formal education.

Sincerely,

Frank Maas

3. Documenting

Letter Requesting Verification of Your College Level Knowledge

The sample letter that follows may be helpful. Take a look at it before you request your letters of verification. Although you'll surely want to revise it to fit your personality and circumstances, you need to be as specific as possible. The more specific *you* are, the better the letter you will receive.

Sample Letter C

Dear _____

As we discussed on the telephone, I am writing to ask you for a letter on my behalf for Diamond College's Portfolio Assessment Program. As you know, I am hoping to earn college credits toward my degree for knowledge acquired outside the college classroom. Your letter will help me provide evidence that the knowledge I believe I possess is worthy of college credit.

Following the recommendations specified by the Assessment Program of the College, I would like your letter to include the following:

1. A description of my position with all pertinent past and present experiences included.

2. A mention of your relationship to me, for example: supervisor, and the situations in which you have observed me. Also, please include the dates of your observations and the length of time I worked with you.

3. An indication of my competence, skills, and knowledge in the following areas: (Here you want to specify what those competencies, skills, and knowledge areas are, and relate them to the course descriptions for which you are seeking credit.)

4. Evaluate how well I performed using such adjectives as average, above average, exceptional, etc. It would also be helpful if your statement included some comparison with others you have known who possess a college degree or college credits and who have held similar positions to mine.

It is important for me to add that what you write should not be a letter of recommendation, per se. Rather, the Assessment

Program requires that you verify my specific skills, competencies, and knowledge and evaluate the level of my performance.

I would appreciate your sending this letter on company (organization) stationery to my advisor at Diamond College, 456 Espirit Street, Newtown, MI 04371. I would like this letter to reach (name of advisor) no later than (allow at least one month from date you write letter).

Thank you very much for agreeing to write this letter on my behalf. As I am sure you are aware, earning a college degree at this point in my life is very important to me.

If you have questions, please let me know.

Thank you once again.

Sincerely,

Your Name

4. *When to Request Documentation.* Since you will more than likely depend on others to provide you with the documentation you need, you want to send your request letters off as soon as possible after you have identified your knowledge. Give your document resource person a deadline of *at least one week prior* to the time you actually will need his/her letter. (You should probably allow four to six weeks.) After a month, you may wish to follow up your written request with a second phone call—just a gentle reminder that your deadline is fast approaching and you will provide any information that will make the job easier for your resource person.

5. *Monitor Your Documentation Requests.* Using a worksheet like the one on the next page will help you avoid last minute problems.

Documentation Supplements

To supplement your direct or indirect documentation, you may want to include job descriptions, in-service training reports, or records of successfully completed courses or workshops for which college credit was not awarded. Although they can be helpful, these documents are generally not enough by themselves to qualify you for credit.

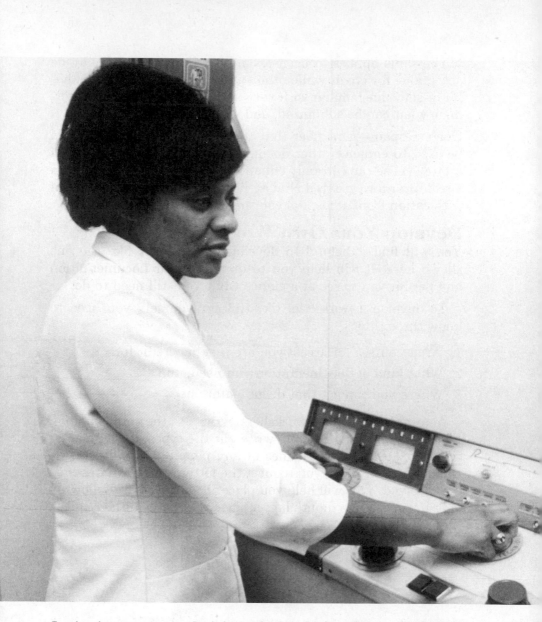

Janice is an x-ray technician who works in a large city hospital. In addition to the nine credits she earned for her knowledge and competence in radiologic technology, she also earned credit for several different courses in psychology and sociology—Marriage and the Family, Gerontology, and Child Development among them. To supplement the learning she gained from her work experience and environment, Janice made use of a t.v. course and non-credit courses offered in her local adult school.

The same applies to licenses and certificates. Some may be acceptable for credit while others may not be. Talk to an advisor or someone familiar with your institution's policies to determine what can be submitted, and what cannot.[1]

Don't despair—remember that the licenses or certificates can be used to enhance other documentation. For example, a real estate license can certainly enhance a letter of verification from a realtor or a Registered Nurse's license will enhance a letter of verification from a hospital coordinator.

Develop Your Own Worksheet

You will find it helpful to develop a worksheet like the one shown here. It will help you to organize your documentation and permit you to see at a glance what you still need to do.

To develop a worksheet like this for yourself, you need to know three things:

1. What courses (or areas) you are seeking credit for,

2. What kind of documentation you need, and

3. Where you can get that documentation.

Across the top of the worksheet, write out the course names. Down the left-hand column, write out the types of documentation you need and the names of any people who will provide them. Note the dates you request the letters and the dates they are received. This will help you place those necessary follow-up calls if more than a month lapses since you made initial request.

---

[1] Many institutions honor the credit recommendations made by the American Council on Education or other agencies regarding military training programs and employee training programs sponsored by various companies and agencies across the country. Check your college catalog or speak with your advisor or the registrar to learn if you can earn credit through this means at your college.

WORKSHEET #2

Monitoring Your Documentation Resources

Types of Documentation	Public Speaking		Accounting		Personnel Mgt.	
	Requested	Received	Requested	Received	Requested	Received
Letters of Verification Mrs. Joan Wilson School Board President	10/1	10/15	10/1	10/15		
Mr. Manuel Gomez Director, Outreach Program Union Community Service Agency	11/3					
Mrs. Ruth Silverstein Director of Personnel Services Union Community Service Agency					11/3	
Program Notes		In office file				
Newspaper articles		In office file		In office file		

The Problem of Knowledge of Competence but No Documentation

There are many areas of knowledge for which people wish to earn college credit but have no documentation of any sort—direct or indirect. Frequent examples of this are languages or humanities fields such as specialized areas of literature. In these cases, if a student has no documentation and if there are no standardized credit-by-examination opportunities in his/her area of expertise, many institutions will arrange for a special evaluation by a selected faculty member in the field.

These faculty evaluators may assess your knowledge through an interview or oral exam, through a written examination, or through a combination of these methods. The results of this evaluation will take the place of documentation in your portfolio. Similarly, if you are seeking credit in an area of the performing arts or a laboratory science, you may be expected to undergo a performance evaluation. In any of these cases, speak with someone at your institution as to your options—there are many ways to get the credit you deserve.

Summary

In this chapter we have focussed on documenting your knowledge, verifying what you claim to know. We have identified two types of documentation—direct and indirect—and have listed the five steps you will need to go through to assemble strong documentation for your portfolio:

- Identifying what you know
- Listing your documentation resources
- Requesting the documentation you need
- Knowing *when* you need to request your documentation, and
- Monitoring your documentation resources.

We also took a brief look at how licenses and certificates can be used in your portfolio and what to do when you have college-level knowledge but no documentation to prove it. In the next chapter we will consider how to organize your portfolio and how to make your credit request.

4.

Organizing Your Portfolio

Write from experience and experience only ... Try to be one of the people on whom nothing is lost.

—Henry James

The Dilemma
Determining Your Credit Request
Selecting Your Documentation
Presenting Your Documentation
Writing the Essay or Narrative
Workshops and Advisors

The Dilemma

Unfortunately, for thousands of adults across the United States who, like you, are working toward earning college credit, there is no single formula to follow. Each institution has its own procedures, policies, forms, fees, and timetables. However, there are several elements that nearly all assessment of prior learning programs have in common:

Determining Your Credit Request

One of your toughest tasks in the assessment process is to figure out how much credit to request. The following approaches are commonly used, although again, you must check with a school representative to make sure you are on the right track.

1. College Course Method

If your institution or the program in which you are enrolled requires you to match your knowledge to specific college courses, much of the burden of requesting the right amount of credit will be lifted from your shoulders. A quick perusal of almost any college catalog will show you how much credit is awarded when you successfully complete a course. If you succeed in demonstrating comparable knowledge through the assessment process, expect to receive a like amount of credit. There are several aspects of selecting courses, though, that you will want to consider. Refer to Chapter II before you begin the search for courses that reflect your knowledge.

It is also important to learn whether or not your institution limits the *kinds* of courses for which you may earn credit. The questions below will help you to gather this information:

- Must the course descriptions only be from your institution's catalog?
- If the descriptions can be from other catalogs, are there particular limitations or restrictions you need to know?
- Must the course descriptions only be in non-major or free-elective areas or can you use credits earned through assessment of your prior learning to demonstrate competency in your major as well?
- Is there a limit on the number of credits or courses you can earn through an assessment of your prior learning?

Get the answers to these questions *before* you begin to assemble your portfolio or undergo the assessment process.

2. Learning Components Method

"Learning Components" is an educational phrase that refers to what you know and what you can do. It permits you to cluster your knowledge in the way you know it. Suppose, for example, that you know something about writing.

—You have worked in an office and know how to write business letters and memos;

—As part of your work with a volunteer agency, you regularly write press releases; and

—Last year, you had a children's story published in a local magazine.

It is unlikely that you will find any one course in business, journalism or creative writing to describe your knowledge and skill as a writer. Your knowledge may be broader or deeper or contain a greater emphasis than you will find in any particular course descriptions.

In this case, "cluster" your knowledge and skills by listing the specific skills, competencies, and accomplishments that reflect your college-level learning. For example, you know how to

—gather information

—determine the important points

—write simply and convincingly

—tailor your writing to the audience and purpose

—create imaginative characters

and you have considerable documentation to prove it! Your next step is to "translate" these learning components into some number of college credits.

Using a College Catalog

One way to do this is to "informally" use an already written college course description (or a set of them). Although you may not be *required* to equate your knowledge to a specific course, the descriptions can be extremely helpful. If you already have experience taking college courses and know in general what is expected in a standard three credit-hour course, you're one step ahead! For example, you took "Principles of Accounting" last year and earned three credit-hours. Now in your portfolio you are requesting credit in banking. You might assign a three credit-hour value to your banking knowledge by recalling what was required to earn the credits in accounting.

College catalogs may be used simply to *compare* your level of knowledge to that detailed in the course descriptions. As you read a particular description, ask youself: do I *know* that, have I *done* that, is that *what my evidence reflects?*

Estimate the percent of knowledge you think you have for each course that touches on your areas of expertise.

Course descriptions, as diverse as they are, are the most readily available fountains of information. They are your first clue to what college faculty expect you to know in a particular field and are excellent tools that should be taken advantage of on your way to your degree.

Calculating College Credit

There is a second method of assigning a credit value to what you know that may be particularly useful if you have attended non-credit courses or workshops. Consider the Carnegie Formula: this formula is a time ratio used by colleges in the United States to calculate college course credit.

A standard three credit-hour course requires students to spend 45 hours of class time and 90 hours of out-of-class work in order to receive credit. In other words, for every 15 hours of instruction and 30 hours or preparation, you earn one credit hour.

For example, suppose you attended a business management workshop two hours each week for 15 weeks, totalling 30 hours of work. You estimate that you spent an additional 60 hours doing assignments and the required readings. With sufficient evidence from this course to support your claim to credit, you could quite legitimately request two credit-hours for this aspect of your portfolio.

While this method may help you estimate what amount of credit to seek, your study efforts must result in learning comparable to that achieved in college courses. The *amount of time* you spend learning something is *not* in itself the evidence of your learning. Your assessor will require evidence, in some form, before being able to make a credit recommendation for your prior learning.

3. Block Credit Method

Some colleges prefer to award "blocks" of credit. In this method, large amounts of credit are awarded based on the depth and breadth of knowledge of someone who has graduated

Mark is a skilled draftsman who has been working for a number of years in a small architectural design firm. As a result of his on-the-job experience, Mark was able to earn credit for his skill in architectural drawing and graphics. Because of his special interest and experience—he and his wife built their own home!—Mark was able to earn additional credits for his knowledge of construction materials, concrete and foundations and electrical systems.

and is employed in a particular field. If you have extensive experience in business management, for example, you might have the equivalent of 24 business credit-hours. To use this method to formulate your credit request, you need to identify general areas of expertise held by professionals in the field and compare your knowledge to theirs.

If your institution uses this method, there should be someone available to help you develop your "block credit request." In some programs, students submit their portfolios to a faculty committee; the committee then makes the credit recommendations. In yet other programs, students are expected to design their own degree programs, requesting assessment credits as part of their learning contracts. If your program falls into either one of these categories, work very closely with your counselor or mentor to identify how you can best use your prior learning. They will help you develop reasonable expectations for yourself in light of your background and experience *and* your institution's policies.

Selecting Your Documentation

As you have read, documentation is critical to your success in earning credit through an assessment of prior learning. Make sure that the evidence presented really does the job it is intended to do, namely, *validate without question* that you possess the college-level knowledge you claim to have. Regardless of your institution's particular method of assessment, you want to insure that your documentation covers several different aspects of your learning. It should:

1. *Describe* your knowledge in as much detail as possible. Look again at the section on "complexity of knowledge and competence" in Chapter 2. Does your documentation help you answer those questions?

2. Show some general *applicability*. For example, knowing the personnel procedures at one organization may be helpful, but does your documentation demonstrate that you could apply your accumulated personnel skills in more than one way?

3. *Relate* to academic disciplines. Your documentation must convey some relation to an academic discipline traditionally taught in college and university classrooms. Look again

at the personal examples given in Chapter 1. Do you think that Sharon could submit pictures of her children as part of her documentation for credit in child development? Why or why not?

4. *Demonstrate* knowledge of theory and application. In many cases, people *either* have theoretical *or* practical knowledge of a given subject area. When you select your documentation, make sure you can demonstrate both. Different subject areas may have different emphases but almost all college-level subject matter contains *both* theoretical and practical components. Does your documentation show both facets of your knowledge?

5. *Verify* your knowledge. Obviously this is what your documentation is all about. Can you explain *how* each piece of documentation verifies *your* knowledge? If you still have questions about this function of your documentation, it would probably be a good idea to review Chapter 3 one more time.

Presenting Your Documentation

It is no secret that the way we present ourselves often tells more about us than the words we speak. Few of us would consider showing up for a job interview at a bank wearing the same clothes we wear to give the dog a bath on Saturday afternoon. The same is true in presenting yourself through your portfolio. Although you may have clearly identified your knowledge and gathered together excellent supporting documentation, the first impression made by the physical appearance of your portfolio will often influence your success in earning the credit you seek. So be sure it looks as good as it should! Here are a few suggestions.

Organize Your Work

Make sure your portfolio is well organized. Following the procedures specified by your own program or institution, group your courses or learning components in a logical, easy to understand way. For example, suppose you are seeking credits in the fields of Principles of Management, Personnel Management, Public Speaking, Group Dynamics, Introduction to Psychology and Business Writing. If you were the faculty committee or faculty assessors responsible for reviewing your portfolio, how would you like to see the portfolio organized?

One possibility would be to group your courses or learning components by general academic discipline:

Management:	Principles of Management
	Personnel Management
Psychology:	Introduction to Psychology
	Group Dynamics
Communications:	Public Speaking
	Business Writing

Chances are that in this example, your public speaking and business writing skills might be related to another grouping. In this case, you would include it with the group that clearly provided you with the most relevant *learning experience.* Alternatively, you may want to include your skills in one group or the other depending on the *documentation* you have. Did your letter written for personnel management include verification of your business writing knowledge? If so, maybe you should include your other documentation for business writing immediately after your personnel management materials. Perhaps your public speaking and business writing skills were developed largely from experience not related to the other documentation in your portfolio. In this case, you would simply present these courses or learning components as separate units.

Don't dwell too much on *how* your portfolio is organized but be sure that it *is* organized. The clearer you organize your work, the easier the reviewer's job is as he or she evaluates your college-level knowledge and skills.

Relate the Documentation to Your Courses or Learning Components. Intrinsic to the assessment process is the need to relate your documentation to your actual knowledge. Nowhere is this more important than in the organization of the portfolio itself. Remember Worksheet #2? It was intended to help you identify the relationship between your knowledge and your sources of documentation. Now you will need to do this in your actual portfolio. One means of showing this relationship is through the preparation of an essay or narrative which will be discussed below.

Another way to assist assessors is by *labeling* each part of your portfolio. Through the use of a table of contents and tabs on the key individual pages of your portfolio, identify which documents verify your knowledge of each course or learning component. Again, *clarity of intent* can only help you. So take the time to carefully *label* your documentation and the course or learning component it is intended to verify.

Be Neat. "Neatness counts" is as true here as it is for all the first graders struggling to print their ABC's. You know yourself how difficult it is to read sloppy handwriting or poorly typed pages. You also know that typographical errors, misspellings, or punctuation errors can lessen the impact of any written message. In your portfolio, you will want to have as strong a positive impact as possible on the assessors. Keep in mind that college-level knowledge, regardless of the subject area, *assumes* a basic competence in communication—writing, in particular. So be sure to prepare your portfolio neatly and accurately. You may need to rewrite some pages. Although it's time-consuming and may be an annoying chore, it's a good idea to revise your work until it is just the way you want it. Always have someone else check your work one last time for spelling, grammatical, typographical, and punctuation errors. Only then can you really be sure that your work will represent you in the best possible way.

Writing the Essay or Narrative

Almost all assessment programs require a general essay or narrative in which you tell something about yourself, your experiences, your goals and aspirations, and your reasons for seeking credit for your prior learning. Although the essay or narrative is frequently not linked as strongly to the actual credit recommendation as is your documentation, it is a very important component because it communicates *who* you are.

College students who attend classes often have an entire 15-week semester to convey to their professors who they are. Through classroom participation, promptness in meeting assignments, research projects and exam grades, professors get a pretty good idea of their motivation, breadth and quality of knowledge, and the level of their communication skills. In most assessment of prior learning programs, you are expected to accomplish all of this on *one* occasion! Doesn't sound like an easy task, does it? Although you may have doubts, an essay or narrative provides you with an excellent opportunity to do just that: show who you are—your motivation, competence, and communication skills. It will also help you put your knowledge and experience in perspective.

Although your institution or program will probably provide you with its own essay or narrative outline, here are a few suggestions for developing this part of your portfolio:

1. *Begin in a straightforward manner,* that is: state your goals and relate them to your reasons for seeking credit for your prior learning, or write a brief description of your learning experiences and how they relate to your portfolio and to your overall educational objectives.

2. *Use a tone that is self-confident and assertive (but not arrogant).* You want to communicate your strengths and accomplishments and also provide a description of your motivation to earn a degree. Are you completing something started long ago or seeking a job promotion? Whatever the motivating factor is for you to want to earn credits through the assessment process, let it come across in your tone.

3. *Organize your essay or narrative in a clear, logical, and comfortable way.* You may wish to organize your essay chronologically by subject matter; whatever feels right to you will probably produce the best results.

4. *Convey what is important.* Naturally, this will depend on what your institution expects. In some instances, institutions seek full autobiographies; in others, only the learning experiences *directly* related to your request for credit are considered important. In either case, make sure you include *everything* that seems relevant or important.

5. *Develop a conclusion.* Make sure that the end of your essay or narrative sums up your intention for earning credits through the assessment of prior learning. Although there is no formula for a perfect conclusion, you will want to make sure yours is consistent with the rest of your text and positive in tone.

   The most impressive essays or narratives convey not only the factors that have contributed to a person's experience or growth, but also some sense of excitement about continuing that experience or growth in a new direction, with greater understanding, or in a more diversified context.

The essay or narrative may seem at first like a difficult, though necessary, task, but it can be one of the most exciting and rewarding experiences of the assessment process. It really does offer you a unique opportunity to reflect on your past, gain a new understanding of yourself and all you've accomplished in your life, and anticipate with confidence your future plans and objectives. The samples provided in Appendix B may be helpful to you as you work on your own essay or narrative.

Remember that by producing more than one draft and then proofreading your essay very carefully, you will come up with a first-class end-product.

"But I haven't written anything in ages...." If it has been some time since you've written a fairly lengthy or important essay, you may want to review or consult *The Prentice Hall Handbook for Writing, The Harbrace College Handbook,* or *Random House Handbook,* which should be available at your public library. If you cannot locate these books, ask your librarian to help you locate others that will serve the same purpose.

Workshops and Advisors

Earlier in this book, we mentioned that many institutions now offer workshops or courses in the assessment of prior learning. As we complete this chapter, we hope it is apparent why such workshops are valuable. Since each institutional program varies, by attending a course or workshop sponsored by your college, you will learn the particulars you need regarding the organization and content of your portfolio, the nature of the evidence considered most valuable, and the expectations for the essay or narrative.

A workshop or course will also provide you with helpful feedback as you compile your portfolio. You won't find yourself working in isolation full of questions and self-doubt. Even if the instructor isn't always available, there may be another student who is having the same documentation problem you are. Perhaps together you can figure out a good solution and present it to the whole class at the next session.

If your institution does not offer a workshop or course in the assessment of prior learning, it probably has advisors or counselors available to help you. Depend on these people to provide you with the information and guidance you need. It is not only their job to do so, but you will find that most advisors and counselors really do enjoy helping others reach their goals!

Summary

In this chapter, we discussed several different models of determining your credit award using

1. The college course model
2. The learning components model and
3. The block credit model

We also focussed on selecting documentation that would most adequately reflect the full scope of your knowledge and skill. We then discussed the importance of preparing your portfolio in an organized, coherent fashion. We stressed the importance of labeling your documentation and relating it to the college courses or learning components for which you hope to earn credit. We also repeated the old adage "neatness counts."

We then described the purpose of the essay or narrative and offered some suggestions as to how you might proceed.

Lastly, we urged you to consider taking an institutional course or workshop in assessment by portfolio and seeking out advisors or counselors who can provide you with the information and guidance you will need.

With two small children to care for, Isabelle is a full-time mother and housewife. She has studied organ for many years and is the principle organist of her church. In addition to earning eight credit hours for her ability as an organist, Isabelle was also able to earn credit for her knowledge of music harmony and theory. She earned an additional three credits for her knowledge of church music.

5.

Bringing
It All Together

Sweet is the memory of past labor.

—Euripides

> **Portfolio Parts:** Cover Page/Table of Contents/Essay or Narrative/Learning Components or Course Descriptions
> **Glossary**

There is no doubt that at this point you have learned a great deal about yourself, your institution's policies, and the assessment process. You have had to make many important decisions regarding

- the content areas to be assessed
- the documents to be included
- the content and organization of your essay or narrative

and dozens of other smaller decisions which have been part of the assessment process. At this last stage, bringing all the pieces together, you will begin to see the interrelationship of all the portfolio parts and to experience the satisfaction that comes in knowing you have done the very best job you could.

Portfolio Parts

The format of your portfolio will probably depend on the policies and procedures of your own program or institution. You will want to follow these carefully. However, most prior learning assessment programs require the following parts:

1. *A cover page.* This should identify your institution and the name of the program in which you are enrolled. It should also contain your name, address, and phone number and include the date that you are submitting your portfolio.

2. *A table of contents.* As in any book, the table of contents will serve to give the reader an overview of the organization of your portfolio and guide him or her to each of the various sections.

3. *An essay or narrative.* This part will provide the assessor with an idea of who you are. As described in Chapter 4, the essay or narrative should show the relationship between your experiences and your college-level knowledge and it should make some mention of your life and educational goals.

   Some institutions will expect you to write a brief narrative for *each* learning component or course for which you are seeking credit. More than likely, a long general essay will not be expected in this situation. Rather, you will be expected to focus on relating your documentation (evidence of your learning) to your knowledge in each, specific area.

4. *Learning components or course descriptions.* In no small sense, this will be the heart of your portfolio. It should identify each learning component or course for which you are seeking credit *and* provide the supporting documentation or evidence. It should also specify the number of credits you are seeking.

If by some chance your institution provides only guidelines but no specific forms for developing a portfolio, you may wish to request permission to use the sample forms that appear in Appendix C of this book.

Once you have assembled your portfolio, make a duplicate copy to maintain a permanent record for yourself before submitting the original to the appropriate college office.

At some colleges, the entire assessment process may be administered by an assessment center. At others, individual departments or instructors supervise the evaluation process of assessment programs or it may be the job of a special faculty group. In any case, when you submit your portfolio, be sure to find out about how long it will take before you hear the results of your assessment. No need to get overanxious too soon!

The day you hand in your portfolio you may experience an enormous sense of relief, and a simultaneous huge surge of exhilaration. When you submit evidence of your prior learning, you also hold up for evaluation a large piece of yourself—quite beyond the physical contents of your portfolio. By presenting yourself and what you know for evaluation, you are demonstrating no small amount of self-confidence, a high degree of motivation, and a willingness to take risks—surely the keys to success in any endeavor!

We wish you well in meeting your life and educational objectives and hope that the assessment process and the college credits earned through it contribute to your success.

*To a great experience one
thing is essential—an
experiencing nature.*

—Shakespeare

GRAND
OPENING
—
HARRY'S
LEMONADE

Harry did not earn credit for his skill and knowledge as a small businessman! He did, however, earn 24 credit hours for his knowledge of acting, directing, scene design, theatrical make-up and technical theatre production, all of which he gained by taking non-credit classes and through firsthand experience in a variety of theatre productions.

Glossary

CAEL: Council for Adult and Experiential Learning is an educational association dedicated to the advancement of experiential learning, fostering its valid and reliable assessment, and sponsoring research and publication on its operation and advantages.

Career Counselor: An individual who specializes in helping people arrive at decisions regarding their career interests, plans, and alternatives.

CLEP: The College Level Examination Program is a standardized credit by examination program offering students the opportunity to earn college credit in many common academic areas. See also ACT-PEP and DANTES.

Computerized Guidance Program: An electronic reference source permitting clarification of values and providing specific information on career alternatives and educational requirements and opportunities.

Correspondence Program: An educational opportunity to complete college courses by working independently though a structured college course syllabus.

Credit: The common United States unit of attainment of college level knowledge or skills.

DANTES: Defense Activity for Non-Traditional Educational Support is a standard credit by examination program offering students the opportunity to earn college credit in many common academic and technical areas. See also ACT-PEP and CLEP.

Department: A group of college faculty and administrators organized by academic discipline.

Documentation: Written or physical proof that is submitted in a portfolio that validates a student's college-level knowledge and skill (also referred to as EVIDENCE).

Evidence: See Documentation.

External Degree Program: An academic degree program which allows a student a number of flexible alternatives to earn college credit and complete a standard 2 or 4-year college curriculum. Since external degrees usually do not have residency requirements, individuals can usually complete degree requirements at their own pace.

Learning Component: A learning component is an element of a larger educational program leading to skills and knowledge in a particular academic discipline.

PONSI: The Program on Noncollegiate Sponsored Instruction of ACE enables individuals to earn college credit for learning acquired outside the sponsorship of colleges and universities. The Program evaluates and makes credit recommendations for formal educational programs most often offered by business, industry, labor unions, professional and voluntary associations and government agencies.

Registrar's Office: The college office responsible for maintaining students' records and issuing transcripts.

Semester: A block of time dividing up a traditional school year, usually four months in length.

Semester Hour: A semester hour is a unit of academic credit usually representing an hour of class (such as a lecture class) or three hours of laboratory work each week for an academic semester, plus related out-of-class study.

Transcript: A listing of all the college courses taken by a student with the credits earned at a particular institution. The imprint of the college seal and authorized signature on the transcript attest to its validity.

6.

Postscript: An Adult Guide to Understanding Colleges

A trip of a thousand miles begins with the first step.

—Chinese proverb

If you are already enrolled in a college, you can probably skip this section. However, if you are considering attending college for the first time or returning after an absence of several years and hope to earn credit for your prior learning, you will want to learn as much as you can about the institutions that are best suited to your needs. The old notion of colleges and universities resembling "ivory towers" still persists in our society but in fact, many colleges and universities have changed considerably over the past several decades. They are more accessible than ever before, offering flexible hours, schedules, and opportunities for earning credit especially designed for adults.

While this book has focussed on the latter—how you can make use of one of the flexible options of earning college credit—assessment by portfolio—this postscript is intended as a short roadmap to help you choose the school best suited to your overall educational needs. As in selecting any other service or product, you may also want to do additional reading. A well-informed consumer is usually the best consumer, even in educational matters.

Knowing Your Goals

As was discussed earlier, knowing and defining your goals are the absolutely necessary first steps to selecting the best college for you. Do you want a bachelor's degree so you will be eligible for a promotion at work? Do you want to make a career change? Are you interested in a specific vocation but unclear about the particulars of the field? Do you want to pursue a lifelong interest without regard to employment? These are some of the basic questions you will want to answer for yourself; the answers will help you identify the type of program or degree you want, and that, in turn, will lead you to pick the best institution.

No doubt, you will also have to consider other very practical matters such as:

- Does a college in my area offer the type of program I need?
- How much does it cost?
- How long will it take?
- Will the certificate, diploma, or degree I receive help me reach my goals?

While obtaining a college degree will not in itself assure you of a better job or higher earnings, it can be one of the most rewarding experiences of your life, particularly if it does help you reach specific goals. If your goals are career-related, it is reasonable to hope that a college degree will provide you with the necessary tools to reach them.

It is not uncommon for people of any age to feel uncertain about their goals—whether they be personal or vocational. Goals can be elusive, especially if our own life circumstances grow more complex and demanding (remember the stories of Jim and Terry in the Introduction?).

Many resources are available today to help you clarify your goals, develop reasonable expectations for yourself, and a plan for helping you reach your objectives. It will be worth investing some time and money in one or more of these resources as you search out the best means of reaching your educational or career goals.

Books are almost always invaluable resources in helping you to clarify or stimulate your thinking. You may want to consult your local library or book store to see what is available.

Titles you may want to consider are:

Robert L. Bailey. *The Career Educational and Financial Aid Guide,* NY: Arco Pub., 1983.

Eleanor Berman. *Re-entering: Successful Back to Work Strategies for Women Seeking a Fresh Start,* NY: Crown Publisher, Inc., 1980.

Richard N. Bolles. *What Color Is Your Parachute? A Practical Manual for Job Hunters and Career Changes,* Berkeley, CA: Ten Speed Press, 1983.

Anna Burke and Mae Walsh. *What Do You Want to Be Now that You're All Grown Up?* Englewood Cliffs, NJ: Prentice Hall, 1982.

John Caple. *Career Cycles: A Guidebook to Success in the Passages and Challenges of Your Work Life,* Englewood Cliffs, NJ: Prentice Hall, 1983.

John C. Crystal and Richard N. Bolles. *Where Do I Go from Here with My Life?* Berkeley, CA: Ten Speed Press, 1974.

Homer R. Figler. *Overcoming Executive Mid-Life Crisis,* NY: Wiley, 1978.

Howard Figler. *PATH: A Career Workbook for Liberal Arts Students,* Cranston, RI: Carroll Press, 1975.

Linda Kline and Lloyd L. Feinstein. *Career Changing: The Worry Free Guide,* Boston: Little, Brown, 1982.

Daniel J. Levinson. *The Seasons of a Man's Life,* NY: Knopf, 1978.

Pam Mendelsohn. *Happier by Degrees: A College Reentry Guide for Women,* NY: Dutton, 1980.

Anne L. Russell. *Career and Conflict: A Woman's Guide to Making Life Choices,* Englewood Cliffs, NJ: Prentice-Hall, 1982.

Gail Sheehy. *Passages: Predictable Crises of Adult Life,* NY: Dutton, 1976.

Often though, reading books about setting goals is not sufficient. Talk with someone, a professional person whose job is to help people define their goals and develop a plan for reaching those goals. Such people are often called educational or career counselors. They may be found in adult schools, high schools, colleges and universities, or through a number of community service agencies such as local "Y's." There are also many educational brokers or consultants who practice privately. These individuals should be listed in the yellow pages under "Career and Vocational Counseling" or "Educational Consultants."*

Before making an appointment to see anyone you will want to speak with that person on the phone to request that information about his or her services be sent to you, or locate a satisfied customer who can give you a positive recommendation about a particular person or agency.

To be effective, career counseling should include:

- an inventory of your skills, abilities, values, and interests
- information on current trends
- the employment needs in your community and throughout the nation

---

* The National Center for Educational Brokering can tell you if there are educational brokers in your area. Write to: National Center of Educational Brokering, Association for Humanistic Sociology, 325 9th Street, San Francisco, CA 94103.

6. Understanding Colleges

- a list of skills, education, and experiences needed for each occupation
- a likely career path and salary scale from entry-level to senior positions in this field
- information on where training or education for the particular career is available

Good educational counseling should include:

- identifying your educational goals
- relating these goals to your career goals
- identifying learning experiences already acquired that relate to educational and career goals
- identifying credit by examination or assessment programs in which you can earn credit for your prior learning
- identifying your preferred learning style, e.g., independent study or taking courses
- identifying costs, commuting distance, and other practical concerns
- developing a plan that is as specific as possible

Computerized guidance programs are also becoming more readily available. Through the use of a micro-computer terminal and user-friendly programs, you will be able to clarify your goals and consider your educational options. Two of the better known computerized guidance programs are called SIGI Plus developed by Educational Testing Service and Discover for Adults, offered by the American College Testing Company. These are often available on college campuses, at libraries, or in career counseling centers.

While it may seem odd to you that a computer—even a user-friendly one—could help you in as personal an area of your life as setting goals and developing an educational plan, computerized guidance systems have been used successfully for many years with young people. Computerized guidance systems permit individuals to work at their own pace, and revise and reconsider responses. Trained counselors are usually available before, during, and after each computerized guidance session, so do not fear that you will be in an isolated room, far removed from human contact. Quite the reverse is true! Computerized guidance systems should be thought of as another tool available to help you determine your goals and devise an educational or career plan.

Regardless of the resources you use, once you have a set of goals and an educational plan, you want to select the institution best suited to your needs. That's what the remaining pages of this book will help you do.

Higher Education Institutions

Keep in mind, as you begin to consider colleges and universities, that no two are exactly the same. Some, for example, have made significant progress in responding to adults' needs. They have introduced many flexible credit-bearing opportunities, extended their programs to include weekend colleges, early morning and late evening course schedules, and developed courses specifically suited to the needs and interests of adults. Some institutions, however, have changed little. If you should approach one of these institutions, do not be surprised if you feel frustrated and disappointed to learn that all courses are offered only during the day, that there are few, if any, opportunities for earning college credit for learning obtained outside the college classroom, and that in general, the programs and services of the college are geared to the educational needs of the 18–22 year-old student. But don't let your frustration or disappointment last too long. As we enter the last decades of the twentieth century, there are hundreds of colleges and universities that will be responsive to your needs. You just need to know where to look.

Types of Colleges

In general, there are three types of degree-granting postsecondary—beyond high school—institutions:

1. *Community colleges or county colleges* are two-year institutions generally supported by state and local taxes and student tuition. As a group, these colleges have been extremely responsive to the needs of adult learners (who are the taxpayers as well!) and offer well-developed programs and services to adults.

Usually located in population centers, community colleges offer several different credentials:

- associate degrees
- certificate programs

- non-credit courses related to professional interests or recreation

Associate degrees are equivalent to two full years of college study or about sixty semester-hour credits (see glossary). The three most common associate level degrees are Associate in Arts (A.A.), Associate in Science (A.S.), and Associate in Applied Science (A.A.S). Depending on your interests and your educational goals, you will be expected to select and enroll in one of these degree programs if you expect to be awarded a degree.

It may be of interest to you to know that two out of every five students who attend college in the United States begin their educations in two-year institutions. This proportion is increasing every year.

One reason for the popularity of community colleges is their open door admissions policy, which means that to qualify for admission you need only to have graduated from an accredited high school or have received an acceptable score on the GED (General Educational Development Test).

A second reason for their popularity is their tuition or fee structure. Generally speaking, tuition charged at community colleges is well below that charged by four-year institutions, whether publicly or privately controlled. Another important reason, especially for adults, is that many community colleges have outstanding testing and assessment programs by which you can demonstrate your prior learning. They also permit you to attend on a part-time basis.

If your ultimate goal is to obtain a baccalaureate (four-year) degree, you can usually take your first two years of study at a community college and then transfer to a four-year institution.

2. *Four-year Colleges* grant baccalaureate—bachelor's—degrees in a wide variety of liberal arts, business, and professional areas. They may be public, private, small or large. Some may also offer associate degrees; some offer graduate programs. Most four year colleges will accept an A.A. or A.S. degree in transfer.

The bachelor's degree is equivalent to four full-time years of study or a minimum of 120 semester hours. The degrees most commonly offered by four year colleges include the Bachelor of Arts (B.A.), the Bachelor of Science (B.S.), the Bachelor of Science in Business Administration (B.S.B.A.), the Bachelor of Nursing (B.S.N), and the Bachelor of Professional Studies (B.P.S.).

Many four year colleges offer opportunities for part-time study and some opportunity for demonstrating your prior knowledge. Some also offer external degrees—that is, an opportunity to earn your degree with a minimum of or no on-site residency required. A few accredited four-year colleges offer *only* external degree opportunities, providing adult students with the maximum of flexibility in meeting degree requirements.

Public four-year colleges—those supported by state and local taxes and student's tuition—are usually more expensive than community colleges but less expensive than privately controlled four-year colleges.

While financial aid is still largely reserved for students aged 18–22, scholarship money is increasingly being made available to adults who are more often part-time. Investigate the financial aid opportunities in your area by directly contacting the college in which you are interested or the Financial Aid Office of your State Department of Education.

3. *Universities,* like four-year colleges, may be publicly or privately controlled. A university is generally composed of numerous separate undergraduate colleges that offer B.A. or B.S. degrees in a wide variety of fields. The opportunity for graduate study leading to a Doctor of Philosophy (Ph.D.) is what most distinguishes a university from a college. Universities are generally larger than most colleges, offer comprehensive academic programs, and often focus their resources on research issues. Many have options for part-time study. Costs are comparable to those at four-year colleges.

Learning About Colleges
To learn about the specific programs and services of colleges and universities in your area or an external degree program outside of your geographic region, telephone or write for a col-

When Virginia retired from her position as assistant treasurer of a large city bank, the one thing she wanted was to complete her college degree. Making extensive use of credit-by-examination and portfolio assessment opportunities, Virginia completed her degree requirements within two years. She had quite a post-graduation party with three grown children and eight grandchildren all sharing in her celebration!

lege catalog. Don't be surprised if you have to wait for what seems like an unreasonable amount of time to receive the catalog—they're usually mailed third class or book rate. (Revise the old adage, "Patience is a virtue" to read, "Patience in dealing with educational institutions is a particular virtue!")

You may want to request catalogs from several different institutions so you can compare their programs and services. (In many larger cities or university towns, a wide array of college catalogs can be found at local libraries. It's a good idea to skim through a few of these before ordering the ones of greatest interest to you.)

The day the catalog arrives, you are faced with yet another unexpected problem: reading it! While the writers of college catalogs surely *intend* to be direct and clear in describing their institutions, oftentimes the results are less than perfect, especially for readers unfamiliar with educational jargon. In addition, catalogs are usually printed at two-year intervals, and because preparing a catalog often takes the better part of a year, some things in a catalog may be out of date by the time you receive it. All of which is to say, if you have specific questions after reading a college catalog, you will want to schedule an appointment with or write to the Admissions Office to request up-to-date information or to have your questions answered.

To help you use the catalog to the best advantage, here are some key phrases and topics you will want to understand:

Accreditation. Within the first few pages of the catalog, you will find information regarding the agencies or associations that have certified that the college or university meets the certain academic and professional standards. Regional accrediting associations monitor the quality of instruction, the types of programs, the accounting procedures, and all other facets of an institution.

Make sure that the institution in which you enroll is properly accredited, both to attest that you will get a good education and because transferring academic credits or degrees earned at a non-accredited college or university is very difficult.

In addition to regional accreditation, many career-related programs required approval by an organization that monitors only instructional programs associated with a specific career field. Nursing, law, library science, journalism, and social work are some examples of fields which receive program-specific accreditation.

Degree Programs

Basic to every college catalog is a description of the degrees awarded by the college. Depending on your goals and educational plan, you will want to examine carefully the requirements of each degree in which you are interested. There are four different levels of degrees offered at U.S. colleges and universities. These are:

Associate degree—This degree is awarded to students who successfully complete the academic requirements of a two-year college program. You can receive this degree from a two-year institution or at the end of a specified two-year program at a four-year college.

Baccalaureate—This degree, often called the bachelor's degree, is granted to students who have met the minimum requirements for graduation from a four-year college or a four-year program at a university.

Master's Degree—You may work for a master's degree after you have received the baccalaureate. The master's degree—usually a Master of Arts (M.A.) or a Master of Science (M.S.)—requires one or two years of course work beyond the baccalaureate.

Doctorate—This degree is the highest academic degree granted in this country. If you wish to earn a doctorate, you should plan on studying three to four years, if not more, beyond the baccalaureate. There are a number of doctoral degrees. The Ph.D. (Doctor of Philosophy) is usually reserved for students who complete graduate-level courses, perform original research, and write the research results in a paper called a dissertation. Among the specialized doctorates are the M.D. (Doctor of Medicine); the J.D. (Jurisprudence Doctorate) for lawyers, the D.M. (Doctor of Ministry) granted by some theological schools; the D.D.S. (Doctor of Dental Surgery); and the Ed.D. (Doctor of Education) for students who complete doctoral academic work in the field of education.

Graduation Requirements. The requirements for graduation are usually listed in two places in a college catalog: the general academic policies section and the description of the major area or concentration. Of particular interest to you as an adult student will be the institution's policies regarding:

- transfer credits
- residency requirements
- credit-by-examination and assessment of prior learning
- currency of credits

It's important to note too, that to receive your degree you will be expected to fulfill general education requirements or liberal arts core requirements and select a major field from which you must take a specified number of courses or build up a specified number of semester hours.

General education or liberal arts requirements usually express an institution's expectations of what you should know in four or five major areas such as science, mathematics, humanities, social sciences and languages. These areas are usually broad enough and include many course offerings from which you will select relatively few to satisfy the requirements. Many institutions encourage adults to demonstrate their prior learning in these areas by offering challenge examinations, credit-by-examination programs or other assessment opportunities. In reading the catalog, note any areas in which you believe you may already to able to demonstrate competency, and check to see whether and how you can demonstrate your expertise.

The requirements of a major simply mean that you focus on a particular discipline by accruing credits in perhaps 10 to 15 courses in that area. Again, you may be able to earn credits in your major through one of the non-traditional options described earlier in this book.

Deciphering and Accruing College Credits

As is described in Chapter 4, credits are based on the Carnegie Formula, a time ratio used by colleges in the United States to calculate their course credit. You will need to consider your family and work responsibilities to determine how many credits or courses you "can take" at any given time.

Some colleges operate on a semester calendar; others on a quarter calendar. The major difference is the length of each term. Colleges on the semester system offer two terms during each academic year. Colleges in the quarter system offer three terms during the academic year. Both semester and quarter programs are modified for summer offerings.

To calculate credits earned and perhaps transferred to an institution on a different credit system, institutions simply translate the credits in this way: for example, three *quarter* hours equate to two *semester* hours. In doing this computation, institutions generally tend to be generous.

Transfer of Credits

Most colleges and universities accept credit transferred from another accredited college or university. However, as you will read, each institution may differ in its transfer policy. Here are some general guidelines to help you determine the transferability of credits you may already have earned:

1. Only courses which are comparable to those offered by the *receiving* institution will be accepted. Generally speaking, skills development courses such as pre-algebra or remedial English will not be accepted in transfer for college credit.

2. Not all technical courses, such as typing or office management, may transfer to a four-year college.

3. Colleges and universities typically accept credit for courses in which you have earned a grade of "C" or better. Some schools will accept all credits if your cumulative grade point average (GPA) is "C" or better.*

4. Not all credits accepted in transfer will necessarily be applicable to the requirements of your chosen degree program.

5. You cannot receive credit for a course twice, even if the course titles are different. For example, you may have taken a course called Introduction to Accounting in 1965 and later, in 1974, when you wanted to brush up a bit, you

---

* To compute your GPA, consider the following: each credit of A is worth four grade points; B, three points, C, two points; and D, one point. Suppose you have three credits of A, which is twelve grade points; three credits of B, which is nine grade points; and four credits of C, which is eight grade points. You therefore have a total of twenty-nine grade points for ten credits. To determine your GPA, divide the number of credits into the number of grade points. The result in this example is 2.90 or a GPA of a little less than a B (3.00).

took Principles of Basic Accounting at a second institution. In all likelihood, only one of these courses would now transfer.

6. Although credits earned twenty or thirty years ago *may* transfer, the receiving institution may expect you to demonstrate the currency of your knowledge by taking an examination or submitting evidence of your recent work. This is particularly true in some business and professional areas.

If you have accumulated many college credits over the years, you may want to schedule an appointment with someone from the Registrations or Admissions Office who can informally give you some idea of the credits that may be accepted in transfer.

Virtually all colleges require a GPA of at least 2.0 (C) for graduation, and many require higher grades to qualify for admission to special programs. Virtually all graduate schools require a GPA of at least 3.0 (B) to qualify for submitting an application, and many require nearly all grades of A (a GPA of between 3.75 and 4.0), especially in the student's major field.

Residency Requirements

The college catalog will usually spell out very directly the number of credits that can be accepted for transfer and the minimum amount of course work that must be taken at the institution from which you expect to earn your degree. In general, a minimum of one year of course work—30 credits—must be taken from the institution awarding the degree. Policies often require that the last year be taken in residence. However, many schools waive or at least reduce the residency requirement for adult students. You will want to read the catalog carefully on this issue. (Most external degree institutions have no residency requirements.)

Financial Aid

As mentioned previously, you may be able to get financial aid, but time and a fair amount of patience (there's that word again!) may be required because, unfortunately, most financial aid programs favor the full-time student.

Undoubtedly, the college catalog will provide you with information about some of the financial aid programs available. You can also call the Financial Aid Office to see if there are any other special financial aid programs for adults, part-time students, women, or for particular professional areas. (Again, keep in mind that the material presented in a college catalog is often one to three years old, so you may be surprised by how much you can learn through a single phone call.)

Other possibilities to explore on your own include:

1. *Federal programs.* For a free student consumer guide on federal financial assistance, write: Department of Education, Division of Postsecondary Education, Office of Student Financial Assistance, Dissemination Branch/Information Section, Room 4661, ROB-3, 7th and D Street, SW, Washington, DC 20202.

2. *State programs.* Write to the Financial Aid Office of your State Department of Higher Education.

3. *Employee Tuition Reimbursement Policy.* Today many employers offer excellent tuition reimbursement plans for employees wishing to continue their educations. You will want to check with the personnel officer of your business, industry, or union to see if such a program is available.

4. *Books.* Your local library may have a number of books or reference materials describing scholarship programs offered by private foundations or associations. Include a stop at your local library as you pursue opportunities for financial aid. One particular book you may wish to obtain is *Paying for Your Education: A Guide for Adult Learners,* published by the College Board. You may order this publication by writing to: College Board Publication Orders, Box 2815, Princeton, NJ 08541.

Your own efforts, in conjunction with the support of the Financial Aid office of the college you wish to attend, can lead you to find the best sources of aid for you.

Comparing Programs

Armed with the catalogs of the colleges in which you are most interested, you will now need to compare programs. Use the following checklist as a guide to help you identify the college best suited to your needs.

Adapting the System to the Part-Time Learner

1. Are classes scheduled at convenient times and places? Can you, for example, get all the courses required for your degree in the evening? If so, will it take you longer to com-

Geoff has been an avid reader all his life. He has had a special interest in 20th century American literature and history. For his knowledge in these areas, Geoff earned 18 credit hours and was able to begin his college program with advanced standing in English and history.

plete your degree? What recourse do you have if you are closed out of a course?

2. Do full-time faculty members teach in the evening? If not, how do the credentials of part-time or adjunct faculty members compare with those of full-time faculty members?

3. Are the essential offices of the college open in the evening, for example: Registrar, Financial Aid, Bursar or Treasurer, Academic Skills Center, library, cafeteria? Do faculty members have evening hours?

4. What methods has the college developed for awarding credit to the part-time student or the individual who cannot regularly attend classes?

5. Are child-care facilities available?

6. Is there adequate parking or campus transportation?

7. Does the Financial Aid office have information about grants, scholarships, and loans for which part-time adult students are eligible?

New Options for Earning Credit

1. How much of your previous college work will be accepted toward your degree? If some of your credits are rejected because of their age, does the college have a procedure for evaluating your current knowledge in those subjects?

2. What policies and procedures does the college have for evaluating your experiential learning—learning you have acquired on the job, in your community, or through volunteer activities, hobbies, travel, or independent reading?

3. Does the college limit the number of credits you may earn through the assessment of experiential learning?

4. How much does it cost to have experiential learning assessed?

5. How long will the assessment process take?

6. What examinations are available in subjects in which you already have knowledge? What is the difference between taking a department challenge examination and a standardized examination such as CLEP? What are the passing scores accepted by the college for CLEP examinations and other standardized tests?

7. Does the college award credit for professional licenses or certificates? For formal military training? For military oc-

cupational designations? For training in business and industry?

8. What are your independent study options? Can you work with a faculty member on a special project of interest to you and receive credit for it?

9. Does the college offer correspondence courses? Will it accept credits for correspondence courses taken at other accredited colleges?

10. Does the college offer televised or other media courses for credit?

Applying for Admissions

One thing you should keep in mind about the application process is that the decision to attend a particular school is not cast in concrete, even after you have started to attend. If you apply to a school, are accepted, register for courses, and then do not like the school—because, for example, the emphasis or focus in your major field of study is not what you expected it to be—you can look for another school. Students in rural areas or small towns may have difficulty finding an alternative institution but can, of course, consider correspondence programs, media courses, and external degree programs. Carefully look over the entrance requirements of the schools you choose. You should remember that most schools have a special set of entrance requirements for adult students, usually defined as students twenty-five years old or older.

You may want to visit the campus to get a feel of the ambience. Catalogs usually include campus maps, and you can take your own tour if you wish. Or call the Office of Admissions and ask whether there are campus tours available for potential students. If you are planning to attend a traditional college, visit when classes are in session. Does whether there are many older students matter to you? How about foreign students? Minority students? If so, and you do not see many, ask your admissions representative why. Assert your right to ask questions. If you are considering enrolling in an external degree college and it is not feasible to visit the institution, you may want to ask the Admission or Alumni Office for the names of previous or current students who would be willing to share their experiences with you. One or two extended conversations with students knowledgeable about the institution will help give you a feel for how well the institution will satisfy your needs.

Basic Admission Requirements

In most institutions, you will need a high school diploma or a GED certificate. In public four-year or community colleges, this may be the only condition for admission because these schools usually have an open-admissions policy. With a restricted admissions policy, a school may insist that applicants have a 2.00 (C) high school average or are in the upper seventy-fifth percentile of their graduating class. Both qualifications are frequently waived for adults, however.

Check the college catalog to see if there is a special re-entry program for adults returning to college and how it alters the entrance requirements. (Colleges and universities do not have a standard definition of adult. By far the most common definition is anyone twenty-five or older who is applying for admission for the first time or who is applying for readmission after an absence of at least four years. The minimum age may vary from twenty-three to thirty. The conditions may be that you must have been out of full-time academic enrollment for at least two months to eight years. Most college catalogs contain the school's definition of adult.)

At four-year colleges and universities and some private two-year colleges, entrance requirements may also include aptitude test results. Aptitude tests are often part of the admissions process in a four-year liberal arts college. Two of the best known aptitude tests are the SAT (Scholastic Aptitude Test) and the ACT (American College Testing) examinations. Again, many institutions waive this requirement for adults. If you have a lot of anxiety about test taking, one of your criteria for seeking admission to a particular school may be whether it requires aptitude test results.

The SAT consists of two sections, and you are allowed one-and-a-half hours for each. The English section measures reading comprehension and vocabulary, and the mathematics section measures your ability to use mathematical reasoning. The test is given several times a year in locations around your state. Any high school guidance counselor will have the dates and times for the SAT and the form you need to fill out and send with your test fee.

The ACT consists of four parts: English, mathematics, social science, and natural science. The ACT is about half an hour longer than the SAT. The cost is roughly the same as the SAT.

ACT is currently conducting research on the performance of adults on this test. A pilot study of about 200 adult women who had returned to school after two to more than twenty years away showed that the average scores for the pilot project were almost identical to the average scores of the incoming freshman class.

College Transcripts

You may obtain copies of your academic record by writing to the registrar of each school you attended.

When you apply for admission, the receiving college needs an official transcript from the institutions you previously attended. You should check to see whether by "official" the school means that the transcript must be mailed directly from one college to the other or whether you may receive the transcript from your old school and then enclose it with your application for admission. To obtain copies for yourself, write to the registrar of each school you attended. Be sure to provide the dates of your attendance and the name or names under which you were registered. There is sometimes a fee of $1 or $2 for each transcript.

At some schools, students can get special permission from the academic dean to start over again, and the school will disregard a transcript that has low marks for course work the student took several years ago. However, in most cases, the work from all previous transcripts is included, which can make recovery of a high grade point average difficult. But do not be discouraged if your transcript does contain some low grades; adult students tend to receive very high marks.

Formal Application

When you request an application form, ask whether there is a special adult admission form. Adult forms tend to be substantially shorter than regular student applications.

The application has a place to list all former education as well as the usual demographic data. For many liberal arts schools you will be asked to write a statement about your life goals and how a college degree fits into these goals, or you may be asked to present and discuss a brief biography of your values and experience. Do not worry unduly about this type of admissions essay. You probably have thought about your goals, your values, and the place of college in your life more deeply and thoroughly than an 18-year old student. Take a look at Chapter 4, Writing the Essay or Narrative, to sharpen your writing skills. The same principles of good writing apply to your admissions essay as to your portfolio essay.

Plan on paying an application fee, even in tuition-free two-year schools. The fee may be anywhere from $10 to $20 and is non-refundable. Application fees to many schools can add up, so you may want to be frugal about how many formal applications you submit.

Admissions Application Check List

Remember to do each of the following when you apply for admission:

1. Send for your high school transcript or your GED test scores in case you need them.
2. Send for transcripts of your academic record at any other institution of higher education you attended.
3. Ask that application forms and financial aid information and forms be sent to you from any institution that interests you.
4. Find out the closest test site for the SAT or the ACT, if they are required for admission.
5. File your financial aid needs assessment form.
6. Send in your application well before the stated deadline to facilitate being considered for financial aid.

Summary

To select the college program best suited to your needs requires several steps:

1. **Clarification of your goals and the preparation of an educational plan. Books and career and educational counselors are available to help you.**
2. **An understanding of the different types of collegiate institutions and the degrees they offer.**

3. Review of college catalogs and key phrases and topics such as accreditation, degree programs, graduation requirements, semester hour, transfer of credits, residence requirements and financial aid.

4. A comparison of the various programs available to you.

5. Applying to the college of your choice.

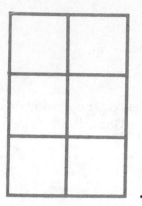

Appendix A

Addresses of Testing Organizations

For information about the various credit-by-examination programs, write to the addresses shown below:

College-Level Examination Program (CLEP)
Educational Testing Service
Princeton, New Jersey 08541

DANTES
Educational Testing Service
Princeton, New Jersey 08541

Advanced Placement Program (APP)
Educational Testing Service
Princeton, New Jersey 08541

ACT-Proficiency Examination Program
(ACT-PEP)
American College Testing Program
P.O. Box 168
Iowa City, Iowa 52243

Ohio University Examination Program
Lifelong Learning
309 Tupper Hall
Athens, Ohio 45701

Thomas A. Edison State College
Examination Program (TECEP)
Office of the Registrar
Att: Mary Bell
101 West State Street CN 545
Trenton, New Jersey 08625

Information about PONSI courses, and licenses and certificates that have been evaluated by the American Council on Education may be obtained by writing to:

American Council on Education
One Dupont Circle
Washington, DC 20036

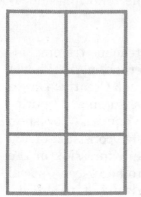

Appendix B

Introduction to Writing Samples

The examples that follow may help you prepare your own narrative or essay. In the first two examples, the students were required to provide information about their knowledge and skills in the specific areas of dance and management. In the third example, the student was required to write an overview of his life and learning. Note that in all three examples, the students gave detailed accounts of their learning experiences and related those experiences directly to the areas in which they were seeking credit.

Before you actually begin to prepare the written portion of your assessment, remember to check with your own institution and review the section in Chapter 4 on writing the essay or narrative.

Narrative for Credit in Creative Dance*

My education and professional work experience in the area of creative dance improvisation is extensive. I have developed a high level of skill in both the teaching and performance of the creative art of expressive body movement. My studies began in 1975 at the Joy of Movement Center in Cambridge, Massachu-

---

* Prepared by Joanna Cashman of Northampton, Massachusetts.

setts where I studied creative dance with Allison Binder and Julie Ince six hours per week for a period of one year. These initial explorations into the art of creative dance affected me very powerfully and positively and prompted the following educational experiences.

In 1977 I participated in a three week teacher training intensive in creative dance with the internationally known teacher/dancer, Barbara Mettler at the Tuscon Creative Dance Center (90 hours of instruction). That same summer I continued my study of dance at the San Francisco dancers Workshop with Anna Halpern. This one month intensive consisted of 120 hours of instruction in creative dance as an expression of the inner life of the dancer and in relationship to her psycho/social and physical environment. In 1979 at the Arizona State University I participated in a three week modern dance workshop given by the members of the Bill Evans Dance Company in which a course in Creative Dance for Children was offered. At the Southwestern School of Behavioral Health Studies in Tucson, Arizona, I participated in a three day workshop which integrated mask making and creative dance expression. In 1980 I traveled to Seattle, Washington, to study with Joan Skinner and the American Contemporary Dance Company at the Skinner Releasing School. Here I learned an approach to creative dance which utilized ideokinetic imagery to release tension and promote access to the subconscious sources of creativity. This three week intensive consisted of 90 hours of instruction.

In 1983 I received a scholarship to attend a progressive three day conference at Baylor College of Medicine in Houston, Texas, called "The Medical Applications of Dance, Yoga and Tai Chi." From 1979 to 1983, I continued my creative dance studies with various faculty members of the Tucson Moving Center.

Through all of these educational experiences, I developed refined artistic sensibilities and craftmanship in the art of creative dance improvisation. My understanding of the elements of time, force, and space was further enhanced by my study of Effort/Shape Analysis at the Institute of Contemporary Dance in Boston, Massachusetts. My own inner process as an artist unfolded steadily as I grew to confidently trust my ability to fuse creation with execution. I learned to tap the stream of the sub-conscious without intellectual censorship, allowing spontaneous and simultaneous exploring, creating and performing. This maturation process led me to the following professional accomplishments.

In 1975, I was invited to become a member of the TA-YU Improvisational Dance Ensemble. We were an eight member professional dance company in residence at the Joy of Movement Center. We performed for one year throughout the metropolitan Boston area.

In 1977 I was invited to join the Barbara Mettler Dance Company in Tucson, Arizona. I felt honored to work with one of America's great dance pioneers and developed considerable skill in group dance improvisation in this 25 member dance company that toured the Southwestern United States. I returned to the Joy of Movement Center as a faculty member in 1978 to teach creative dance to adults.

Upon returning to Arizona in 1978, a number of exciting performing and teaching opportunities were presented to me, including two television appearances. As a guest artist on the Jim Ferguson Show on KGUN TV, I performed interpretive dance of childrens' stories and on KUAT TV I danced in a program called "Dance Probe" which was made possible by a grant from the National Endowment of the Arts and the Arizona Humanities Council. From 1979 to 1983 I was employed as director, dance company and faculty member of the Tucson Moving Center, a non-profit creative arts organization. In this context, I explored, adapted and developed teaching and performing skills with many diverse groups. I performed and taught workshops in creative dance throughout Arizona in a variety of health care, educational and correctional settings including the following.

The Arcosanti Arts Festival
Miles Exploratory School
Assoc. for Humanistic Psychology Conference
Tucson Arts Festival
University of Arizona
The Invisible Theater

Arizona School for Deaf and Blind

Fort Grant Prison

Congress St. Arts Festival

American Friends Service Committee Gala Performance

Arizona Woman's Caucas for the Arts

Very Special Arts Festival

Unity of Man Conference

Sopori School

The Bethasada Players

The Steve Halpern Concert

Unitarian Universalist Church

During this time I also founded and directed "Get High on Dance," a weekly multimedia dance jam for people of all ages. This event provided creative dance instruction, performance, and play opportunities in an environment that was free from cigarette smoke, alcohol, shoes, and expressive movement restrictions. I have enclosed documentation to support this narrative. I feel that my education and experience in the field of creative dance improvisation far exceeds that of a one semester college course in depth, breadth, and practical application. I am requesting 9 credits for 9 years of activity in the field of creative dance as student, performer and educator.

Narrative for Credit in the Management Process*

I have been a member of the administrative team of the Masonic Home since September, 1978. I have served as the Directress of Nursing Service and in my present position as Assistant Administrator/Professional Services. Job descriptions and responsibilities are attached as evidence (A).

Our table of organization (evidence B), outlines the scope of my responsibility and the coordination required to manage each department.

On February 2, 1982, I attended a special invitational conference entitled "Management in Long-Term Care Facilities." The purpose of the conference was to improve the leadership skills of administrators in long-term care facilities. Our objectives were to 1) discuss the management concepts of cost effective

---

* Prepared by Barbara Fels of Clarksburg, New Jersey.

care, unionization, decentralization, competency based evaluation, evaluation of nursing services, and competition for health
care services; 2) outline the historical aspects of management in
nursing homes; 3) understand some of the political aspects of
nursing home administration; 4) state the administrative tal-
ents needed by long-term care administrator, currently and in
the future; 5) discuss the trends in long-term administration;
and 6) identify felt needs for program content on management
theory for two future conferences. Attached as evidence (C) are
my letter of invitation and confirmation of enrollment.

On November 9, 1981 I completed a six hour seminar on
"Handling Staff Problems" given by Geriatric Educational
Consultants. The speakers were Stephen M. Holden, Ph.D and
Steven E. Perkel, MA, ACSW. Our achieved objectives were to
analyze staff problems, assess organizational structure and its
impact on staff relationships, to define their own role in building
performance standards, increase staff motivation, utilize techniques to minimize intra-staff friction and apply effective prob-
lem-resolution methods. Attached as evidence (D) is certificate
of attendance.

I attended a seminar on September 23, 1983 on "Making Performance Evaluations Really Work." It was designed to teach
managers the value and method of writing performance standards and objectives so they could conduct more beneficial
performance appraisals. Our objectives were to 1) identify appropriate criteria upon which to evaluate an employee; 2) create
standards of performance; 3) describe an understanding of the
relationship between a job description, procedure manual and
standards of performance; 4) recognize three categories of objectives; 5) define four criteria of a well-stated objective; 6) ver-
balize an understanding of the dynamics in appraisal interviews;
and 7) summarize steps to improving employee performance.
Attached as evidence (E) is my certificate of attendance.

From February 22, 1983 to March 22, 1983 I attended the
Management Course presented by The Management Institute
from Glassboro State College on Supervisory Training. We used
the textbook, *Supervision-Concepts and Practices of Management,* by Haimann-Hilgente. Course content included: 1) The
Role of the Supervisor—the Supervisor's functions and responsibilities, leadership styles and impact and assessing your mana-

gerial style; 2) Working with People—understanding employee motivation and behavior, improving productivity and evaluating employee performance; 3) Maintaining Sound Human Relations—communicating effectively, job orientation, administering discipline, handling complaints and grievances; 4) Problem Solving for Supervisors—absenteeism and other personnel problems, developing more effective relationships with your supervisors and effective use of information; 5) Developing Supervisory Skills—managing your time, setting and achieving work priorities, building an effective work team and effective employee meetings; and 6) Coping with Government Regulations—avoiding discrimination, safety and OSHA, workers compensation laws and current labor laws. Attached as evidence (F) is my certificate of attendance.

I also participated in the advanced course in Management Training on March 27, 1984 and April 3, 1984 given by The Management Institute at Glassboro State College. We used the book *Behavioral Insights for Supervision* by Reber and Van-Gilder. The course content included: 1) Dealing Effectively with Other Managers—group decision making, commitment for joint action and promoting inter-departmental cooperation; 2) Management of Self-Situational Leadership—time management and communications; 3) Management of Subordinates—participating management, communications guidelines, performance evaluations and problem employees and 4) Management of Change—planning for change, preventing the crisis and guidelines for change management. Attached as evidence (G) is my certificate of attendance.

Sample General Essay*
While I was in high school, the recurring question was "what college do you want to attend?" I was never asked whether or not college was in my plans. Well, at the time, I knew that furthering my education in a formal way was not an immediate goal. I saw plenty of opportunity in my working world and was eager to participate in it.

---

* Prepared by James Herrity and reprinted here from *Earning College Credit for Prior Experiential Learning,* a publication of the Vermont State Colleges by Kenneth J. Laverriere, 1983.

Appendix B

The first few years out of school were spent working odd jobs around Lyndonville, Vermont. In April, 1973, when Troll Press (a small print shop) hired me, I knew my decision to bypass a college education had been the right one: I worked with stimulating people, learned and practiced photography, and even had a hand in determining company practices and philosophy. As my photographic knowledge increased, I began to accept free lance photographic work. My commissions grew and spurred a desire to open my own studio.

The Focal Point (as my studio is called) opened in April of 1977. Business steadily increased and continues to do so today. So why am I here? I worked hard, achieved a modicum of success in my craft, and became financially independent. Yet during the last couple of years, I've had a yearning to return to school. It has been ten years since my high school graduation and now I see the need for a more formal education than I've achieved on my own. I have enjoyed my career thus far, but feel frustrated when I envision the limited career possibilities I have with my present education and the whole realm of complex ideas that I cannot enter alone. In short, supporting myself with photography for the rest of my life is not enough. Photography began as a hobby, and I look forward to the day when it is a hobby again.

In January, 1981, I enrolled at Lyndon State College with the intention of graduating with a B.S. in Business Administration and continuing on to law school. Because of past job experiences and the successful operation of my business, I feel I have accumulated a certain amount of knowledge pertinent to the business world. The credits I deserve and request would shorten the long road ahead of me. My experience will speak for itself.

After high school, my first job experience was at a paper mill, where I was low-man on the totem pole in the sheeting department. As helper to the rotating operator on the large sheeting and trimming machines, I was not only kept busy, but content as well because the job varied from day to day.

Due to a slowdown in the sheeting department, I was shifted to yard work. It took about three days to get bored with unloading boxcars and picking up trash, so I began going down to the maintenance department every morning, hoping to be assigned as a helper to one of the maintenance operations. This too was enjoyable: I would alternate between helping plumbers, electricians, machinists, masons, welders, and dam builders. At 18 years of age, I was learning the basics of many different professions.

Soon the union found out that I was not performing my "proper" job and returned me to the yard. After only two days, I quit.

That fall, after spending the summer hiking in the White Mountains, I learned dry wall taping and began subcontracting work on area houses—my introduction to business. It was a loose operation (I'm not requesting credits for the experience), yet I learned from the work. The job entailed estimating dry wall surface area; translating this into materials needed and man hours spent; equipping my four-man crew with tools and training; quoting costs; and being responsible for the finished product. The winter of 1973 brought a slowdown in construction in the area, and to keep their own crews busy, contractors did their own dry wall work. I was out of business.

About a month later, however, I met Greg Guest, the proprietor of Troll Press. Our conversation turned to paper: I'd been making it; he'd been printing on it. Don't be surprised, when one considers texture, weight, finish, curve characteristics, grain and size, there's plenty to converse about. After I told him I was an amature photographer, Greg mentioned he once did photography for a newspaper. He also said his shop was working on a 250 page routing guide for St. Johnsbury Trucking Company, and he offered me the chance to try my luck at shooting the pages at the rate of fifty cents per page. I grabbed the opportunity. When the job was complete, he figured my hourly rate was eleven dollars per hour and offered me a full time job; I was no longer paid by "piece work."

Troll Press was the foundation of both my photography and business careers. At Troll, lithography was my main interest, but because of the company's size and collegial philosophy, I was called upon to participate in other areas of operation.

When I arrived, Troll had three employees; when I left, it had eight. Decisions on such things as equipment purchases, salaries, job descriptions, employment, vacations, expansion, advertising, and marketing were discussed and voted upon by all members of the organization. This corporate experience later helped me resolve similar problems in my own business.

It was at my suggestion that Troll now does its own bookkeeping and accounting, keeping all important data under constant review and control. Troll's books were being kept out of house until my mother (a well-respected accountant) and my father (an equally respected lawyer) stressed to me the importance of knowing efficient accounting operations. My mother showed us the proper techniques and kept an eye on the accounting for a year, until she was confident we would be successful on our own. It was this experience that introduced me to the principles of accounting.

At the Troll I was involved with design of various brochures, press operation, finishing operations and high-volume Xerox operation. I would arrive at work at 7:00; others arrived at 9:00, but I could do more darkroom work in the uninterrupted two hours before 9:00 than at any other part of the day. It was an exhilarating time; I was learning so much.

One morning I was horrified to see that the building was partially burned. Although Troll suffered no fire damage, the water damage was devastating. We immediately began drying, oiling, and removing machinery. There was more work than we could do; it was gratifying to see how many friends our small operation had. Insurance negotiations began immediately, and I played a vital part in estimating damage, tallying inventory, and negotiating the settlement.

My new job was to secure a suitable building for relocation. At first, I had a hard time convincing real estate dealers that I was a legitimate customer (I was only 20) for buying or leasing a large industrial building. We were racing against time: it was summer (our busiest season), and every day the presses were idle, we lost money. Finally, I found a perfect building and called Greg in to see what he felt. He agreed and took care of the financing, while, with production flow in mind, I began designing the plant layout. We were back in operation within two months of the fire.

As our own business grew, we began to experience production coordination problems, which we alleviated through the formulation of new production charts and forms. These enabled us to better estimate completion times and to keep track of the progress of all jobs in house.

In the printing industry, especially in a small community, one is closely involved with customer's advertising and marketing campaigns. We were often consulted for decisions along these lines, and were partially responsible for educating many of the area businesses on these aspects of their operations.

At Troll I gained confidence in my ability to deal effectively with photography, business, and customer relations. It was this confidence that spurred me on to founding my own business.

In April, 1976, the Focal Point opened its doors. Business was slow at first—an asset—for there was plenty to do "setting up" the enterprise. Here I learned about such things as capital financing and the legal aspects of the business world. My parents were again instrumental in teaching me new skills. Indeed, I was fortunate: neither legal nor accounting consultations (in my opinion, the two most important aspects of business) cost the Focal Point a cent.

In my years of running the business, I have had to apply for both long and short-term financing, so I've had to prepare financial statements, analyze net worth, compute costs of sales, determine profit margins and make business projections to justify the creditor's investment in my operation. By analyzing such figures, I was able to determine any needed changes in prices, products or sales target areas. Yet, work was not all glamour: I had to learn proper posting and filing techniques along with effective billing and collection procedures. Any busy photographic studio accumulates thousands of negatives which must be filed so as to be immediately retrievable in event of an order; keeping track of negatives is a "chore" at best.

Obtaining new business is another important function in a successful business. To cultivate my smaller accounts (weddings, portraits, aerials), I advertised in newspapers and on radio stations, sent direct mailings, and exhibited my work at banks and other "high traffic" areas around the community. My larger accounts (commercial, industrial, and fashion) were obtained by direct solicitation and written quotations and bids.

Running my business has been a continuing learning process. Let me stress that when dealing with commercial accounts, both the photography and printing businesses, one learns so much about how other businesses run: one is always dealing with commodities and how to market them. In fact, I picked up the book *The World of Business* by Dan Steinhoff (the text used for "Introduction to Business" at Lyndon State College) just to see if I understood most of the basic concepts explained. I was leery when I saw a few chapters on "big business"; how could a two-person operation know anything about "big business"? Well, I was amazed that all the concepts were ones I had been exposed to on a day-to-day basis such as dealing with marketing executives, advertising directors, salesmen, and presidents of accounts, like Vermont American Corporation, Burke Mountain Recreation, EHV Weidman, and St. Johnsbury Trucking.

Besides photography, I have offered other services to my customers. Business slows down from January to May each year, so I prepare income taxes for both individuals and businesses. The experience of keeping my own books and preparing my own taxes taught me enough to prepare those of others. I kept abreast of changes in regulations by subscribing to various yearly tax manuals; any legal or accounting questions encountered are discussed with either or both of my parents.

As another service to my customers, many of whom are amature photographers, I began two years ago offering organized classroom instruction on camera operation and visual composition. It is through these four-week courses that I learned and used public speaking skills. I have also lectured on photography in college and high school classes and at organizations such as the Rotary. I have recently accepted a position this fall at Lyndon State College teaching the most advanced photography course.

Because both the photography and business worlds are ever changing, I attend seminars on both subjects. The most significant seminars were as follows: the 1979 New England Institute of Professional Photography (offered through Continuing Education programs at the University of New Hampshire) covered new portrait techniques and accounting methods used for photography studios; the 1980 N.E.I.P.P. explained wedding photography techniques and how to establish and implement successful marketing campaigns, and the Essex Photographic Workshop in 1980 taught natural light portraiture. Because these seminars were so stimulating, whenever I returned from one, I could not wait to try the photographic and business ideas and techniques learned. I had a sense of surpassing my own standards; the efficiency and creative quality of my work increased rapidly.

When I started the Focal Point, I had no formal photographic education, nor had I ever seen a professional photographer work. Yet the thirst for knowledge was present, so I spent many hours reading about and practicing technique. When I encountered a problem that was not covered in any of the volumes in my personal photographic library, I would consult technical representatives, colleagues or anyone I thought could help. My knowledge increased rapidly because I have never been ashamed to admit that I didn't understand a certain procedure. For example, in 1979 I entered my first Vermont Professional Photographers Convention print competition. Out of the four prints I entered, only one earned a third place ribbon; in 1980, however, I entered eight prints and won four first place ribbons, two second place ribbons, and the George Reed Memorial Trophy (awarded for the print which most exemplifies Vermont). The 1980 showing placed me in the top five percent of the hundred and three New England professional photographers who entered. As result of the event, publicity in the local papers, I acquired two new accounts, each of which increased my net sales by over three thousand dollars.

Along with what one considers typical studio jobs (weddings, portraits, school accounts, and commercial work), I have also worked on numerous magazine articles and newspaper reports, the most exciting of which was coverage of the U.S. Cross Country Ski Championship for the Associated Press. It was my first job for AP, and I was really nervous. AP representatives from Boston set up a laser photoscanner in my darkroom for the week-long races. My job was to photograph each event, concentrating on shooting those whom I felt were the "favorites."

Upon completion of the last race of the day (usually 4 P.M.), I would rush to the studio, rapidly process the film and prints, compose captions and (via the scanner and telephone) "call" the prints to the AP central office in New York City. The next day, I would have the satisfaction of seeing my photographs in all major newspapers. The feeling was great!

I continued doing feature stories, both of national and local interest, for AP. One "national release" AP story I photographed on poverty in the Northeast Kingdom caused quite a bit of controversy in this area. As opposed to *Vermont Life* approach (pristine Vermont), this article dealt with the poverty and problems in the area and possible solutions. I was condemned for reporting a story which people did not want to hear. (I have, by the way, also taken the other position. I regularly contribute to *Vermont Life* and have been published five times there.)

Free lance journalism is one of the areas I enjoy most, although I don't feel I could be a full-time staff photographer on a newspaper for long: I enjoy choosing the nature of the article to report. Although I am winding down the studio to pursue other interests, I will not have to liquidate any of the studio's assets. Therefore, in the future, to help supplement my income while attending school, I will continue submitting free lance articles to various publications.

Besides being involved in photography, I began bartending at the Old Cutter Inn in East Burke, Vermont in May, 1978. The job quickly entailed more than tending bar: I was head bartender and liaison between the help and the chef-proprietor. Because of my printing and advertising experiences, I helped the owner design his brochures and menus and also had a part in deciding lounge entertainment and menu content. After a year and a half, because the studio was demanding more and more of my time, I had to terminate tenure. The Old Cutter Inn is a quality restaurant, and I enjoyed being a part of it.

Lyndonville has a housing shortage because many Lyndon State College students prefer to live off-campus. So in January, 1978, I purchased a large home in the Village which I financed by renting rooms to college students. Here, again, I feel this was an experience which helped tune my business expertise.

Another aspect of my life I am proud of is my work for the Fenton Chester Ice Arena. As a small community, we are fortunate to have a recreation facility of its size and quality. From the beginning, I have been involved in both fund-raising and the design of the facility. I was an active member on the board which revised and finalized the architect's plans, and in April, 1980, I was elected Vice President of the organization. My present duties there include price setting, scheduling, promotion, employee relations, maintenance schedules, expenditure appropriations and cost analysis. When I was first elected to the board of directors, I felt intimidated because I was so young compared to the other members. Yet once I realized that being elected showed the members' confidence in my capabilities, I dug in and became zealously involved.

While the organization is solvent, I feel, along with other board members, that the facility must have an "off season" use to remain self-supporting. So last summer, I started an annual farmers' market at the Arena. I am also on the committee in charge of scheduling and promoting dances and concerts to be held this summer.

Last night, at the Arena's annual corporator's meeting, I ran for Treasurer and was elected. I felt the books were not being well kept. Vital information was not always available at meetings from the Treasurer, probably because of an inadequate accounting system. The Arena is a $500,000 facility and warrants an extensive, complete accounting system which I look forward to implementing.

The first year the arena opened, I founded the Lyndonville Youth Hockey Association, which took countless hours of fund-raising and promotion. Our first year we had 27 participants. This year we had grown to 63 skaters. In the beginning, I did all the scheduling, bookkeeping, equipment purchasing and registering, but because of the anticipated growth, before the second season started, I asked for help and was grateful to receive offers from many parents. The organization is well on its way now to being a fine one. I'm glad to say I am no longer running it, but remain on the board of directors.

I spend most of my time coaching the kids, which I enjoy most. I get along well with kids and have fun working with them. I get such a feeling of accomplishment when I watch their progress. We teach the youngest age group (4-7 years old) skating by having them push chairs around the ice. Last year one little boy was having an awful time. The chair acted as added stability with most kids, but this particular boy was so inept at keeping his balance on skates that he not only fell down, but also dragged the chair down on top of him, thus trapping himself. I rushed over thinking "Boy, this kid is going to call it quits" but he didn't and now he cruises around the rink like all the other kids. It's amazing how much one can learn from children.

In the last ten years, I have pursued my photographic and business interests along with community volunteer work. I feel I have matured through all my experiences, both good and bad. The change I now need stems from a feeling that my life isn't fulfilling enough. When I meet someone and they learn I am a photographer, I always get the same reaction: "What a great way to make a living." Well, although I have enjoyed the profession, I am beginning to tire of taking other people's pictures. I have been in college for a semester now and look forward to learning more, especially in general education (history, philosophy, literature).

For all the "learning experiences" I have had, from printing and accounting to photography and business management, I still feel uneducated in many ways. While I have a lot of factual and practical knowledge, I don't yet have a larger framework within which my craft and experience become meaningful in the larger sense of the word. I now need a more complex language—new categories of experience—into which I can grow and out of which I can form new goals. In some ways it's ironic that my experience had limited me insofar as I've already achieved a certain expertise in areas of practical knowledge, yet don't possess the tools to interpret the worth of my knowledge or experience.

Law is an interest I have always had (must be from my father), and I feel it is not only a profession which combines the practical and the ideal, but one which is central in understanding our society, the world, and the complex relation between the two. The educational training needed to pass the bar exam will both stimulate my growth and make me a more "well-rounded person" intellectually.

When good friends hear of my intention to go to law school, they greet the idea with skepticism: for them, law, photography, and printing are unrelated. Yet in the larger scheme of things, my life experience thus far and law are complementary: freedom of the press and the traditions of common law have gone hand-in-hand for centuries. I know a good deal about the press, and when I combine that with my future education, I will have an interesting career. Any credits I receive through this course will make the long but exciting road ahead a bit shorter. Thank you for reviewing my request.

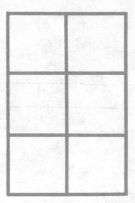

Appendix C

Sample for Your Portfolio

Prior Learning Assessment Cover Sheet

Name of Institution___ DIAMOND COLLEGE_____

Address___ 456 ESPIRIT STREET_____

_____ NEWTOWN, MI 04371_____

Name of Assessment of Prior

 Learning Program_____ PORTFOLIO ASSESSMENT PROGRAM_____

Contact Person_____ MS, PHYLLIS COULTER_____

Your Name_____ JOHN BROWN_____

Address_____ 27 CURRANT LANE_____

_____ LINDENHURST, NY_____

Home Phone____ (403) 671-3210_____

Business Phone (403) 872-1000 x 342_____

Date you are submitting your portfolio____ FEBRUARY 16, 1985_____

C.i

Appendix C

Applicant's Signature Form

I hereby acknowledge that the information submitted is true and correct to the best of my knowledge. Willful failure to give accurate information is considered adequate grounds for dismissal from __DIAMOND COLLEGE__ or for revocation of credits granted as a result of falsified information.

__John Brown__   __FEBRUARY 14, 1985__
(your signature)   (date)

State of __NEW YORK__
County of __SUFFOLK__

I, __MARJORY PRATT__ , a Notary Public, hereby certify that the individual whose signature appears above appeared before me on this date, who being duly sworn, state that the information given herein and attached hereto is true and correct.

My commission expires: __MARCH 1986__ __Marjory Pratt__
(signature)

Notary Public __SUFFOLK__ County

__NEW YORK__ State or Commnwealth

Notary must provide stamp or seal.

c.ii

College Credit for What You Know

<u>SAMPLE</u>

<u>Table of Contents</u>

c.iii

Appendix C

Credit Claim Form

(Use a separate credit claim form for each learning component or course for which you are seeking credit).

Name __JOHN BROWN_____ Social Security Number 999-00-1111

I am seeking credit for the following learning component or college course

  (circle one)

_____JOURNALISM_____

If you are using a course title, attach a photocopy and provide the following information:

  Name of Institution__PRIMROSE UNIVERSITY_____

  Department_____JOURNALISM_____

  Year of Catalog___1985_____

I am seeking __3__ credit hours for this learning component or course.

                                        (circle one)

[x] I am submitting evidence in support of this credit claim. It includes:

a. Letter of verification from Mr. Harold Abbott, current employer
b. Letter of verification from Mrs. Gloria Leo, past employer
c. Examples of articles I have written during the past two years
d. Journalism commendation I received

[ ] I do not have physical evidence in support of the credit claim and am
     requesting a special assessment.

                        c.iv

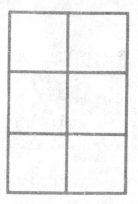

List of Institutions

Colleges Offering Assessment of Prior Learning Opportunities

Each of the colleges listed in the following pages is known to have policies in place for recognizing prior learning. You will want to write or telephone for specific information about the various programs and services of each institution that interest you.

You may also find that an institution you know of has a prior learning assessment program and is not contained in this listing. If so, please let us know!

Lastly, throughout the country, the Council for Adult and Experiential Learning (CAEL) maintains a dedicated field staff who are available to help you find additional educational resources in your region of the country. You may wish to write to CAEL to obtain the names and addresses of these field staff. To do so, write:

CAEL, 10840 Little Patuxent Parkway, Columbia, MD 21044

Again, we wish you success in meeting your educational and life goals. We would be interested in learning if this book proved helpful to you and would welcome your suggestions as to how it could be improved. We would also enjoy hearing of your experiences in seeking credit for your prior learning and your success in earning those credits! Do write.

Opportunities for Credit

ALABAMA

Alabama State University
915 South Jackson Street
Montgomery, Alabama 36195

Alexander City State Junior
College
P.O. Box 699
Alexander City, AL 35010

Athens State College
Beaty Street
Athens, AL 35611

Auburn University, Montgomery
Atlanta Highway
Montgomery, AL 36193-0401

Bessemer State Technical
College
P.O. Box 308
Bessemer, AL 35021

Gadsden State Junior College
#1 State College Boulevard
Gadsden, AL 35999-9990

George Corley Wallace State
Community College
P.O. Drawer 1049
Selma, AL 36702-1049

Hobson State Technical
College
P.O. Box 489
Thomasville, AL 36784

Huntingdon College
1500 East Fairview
Montgomery, AL 36106

Jacksonville State University
Jacksonville, AL 36265

Jefferson State Junior
College
2601 Carson Road
Birmingham, AL 35215-3098

Livingston University
Station 25, LU
Livingston, AL 35470

Miles College
P.O. Box 3800
Birmingham, AL 35208

Mobile College
P.O. Box 13220
Mobile, AL 36613

Northwest Alabama State
Junior College
Route 3 Box 77
Phil Campbell, AL 35581

Oakwood College
Huntsville, AL 35896

Opelika State Technical
College
1701 LaFayette Parkway
P.O. Box 2268
Opelika, AL 36803-2268

Patterson State Technical
College
3920 Troy Highway
Montgomery, AL 36116-2699

Shelton State Community
College
1301 15th Street East
Tuscaloosa, AL 35404

Southern Union State Junior
College
Roberts Street
Wadley, AL 36276

Troy State University
University Avenue
Troy, AL 36082

University of Alabama,
University
P.O. Box CD
University, AL 35486

University of Alabama,
Birmingham
University Station
Birmingham, AL 35294

University of North Alabama
P.O. Box 5121
Florence, AL 35632-0001

Opportunities for Credit

University of South Alabama
307 University Boulevard
Mobile, AL 36688

ALASKA
Alaska Pacific University
4101 University Drive
Anchorage, AK 99508

Anchorage Community College
2533 Providence Drive
Anchorage, AK 99508-4670

Kenai Peninsula Community
  College
Box 848
Soldotna, AK 99669

Kodiak Community College
Box 946
Kodiak, AK 99615

Sheldon Jackson College
Box 479
Sitka, AK 99835

ARIZONA
Arizona State University
Tempe, AZ 85287

Cochise College
Douglas, AZ 85607

College of Ganado
Ganado, AZ 86505

Eastern Arizona College
600 Church Street
Thatcher, AZ 85552-0769

Maricopa Technical Community
  College
108 N 40th Street
Phoenix, AZ 85034

Northern Arizona University
P.O. Box 4103
Flagstaff, AZ 86011

Northland Pioneer College
1200 Hermosa Drive
Holbrook, AZ 86025

ARKANSAS
Arkansas College
P.O. Box 2317
Batesville, AR 72503

Arkansas State University
State University, AR 72467

Harding University
Box 931, Station A
Searcy, AR 72143

Henderson State University
Arkadelphia, AR 71923

John Brown University
Siloam Springs, AR 72761

Mississippi County Community
  College
P.O. Box 1109
Blytheville, AR 72315

North Arkansas Community
  College
Pioneer Ridge
Harrison, AR 72601

Ouachita Baptist University
Box 3743
Arkadelphia, AR 71923

Southern Arkansas University
Magnolia, AR 71753

University of Arkansas,
  Fayetteville
Fayetteville, AR 72701

University of Arkansas,
  Little Rock
33rd and University Avenue
Little Rock, AR 72204

University of Arkansas for
  Medical Sciences
4301 West Markham
Little Rock, AR 72205

University of Arkansas for
  Medical Sciences, College
  of Nursing
4301 West Markham, Slot 529
Little Rock, AR 72205

Opportunities for Credit

CALIFORNIA
Allan Hancock College
800 South College Drive
Santa Maria, CA 93454

American River College
4700 College Oak Drive
Sacramento, CA 95841

Biola University
13800 Biola Avenue
La Mirada, CA 90639-0001

Cabrillo College
6500 Soquel Drive
Aptos, CA 95003

California Baptist College
8432 Magnolia Avenue
Riverside, CA 92504

California College of Arts &
  Crafts
5212 Broadway
Oakland, CA 94618

California School of
  Professional Psychology
2152 Union Street
San Francisco, CA 94123

California State College
9001 Stockdale Highway
Bakersfield, CA 93311-1099

California State Polytechnic
  University
3801 West Temple Avenue
Pomona, CA 91768

California State University,
  Chico
Chico, CA 95929

California State University,
  Northridge
18111 Nordhoff Street
Northridge, CA 91330

California State University,
  Sacramento
6000 J Street
Sacramento, CA 95819-2694

Chaffey College
5885 Haven Avenue
Alta Loma, CA 91701-3002

Chapman College
333 North Glassell Street
Orange, CA 92666

Coastline Community College
11460 Warner Avenue
Fountain Valley, CA
  92708-2597

Cogswell College
10420 Bubb Road
San Francisco, CA 95014

College of the Desert
43-500 Monterey Avenue
Palm Desert, CA 92260

Compton Community College
1111 East Artesia Boulevard
Compton, CA 90221

Consortium of the California
  State University
Academic Program Office
6300 State University Drive
Long Beach, CA 90815

Contra Costa College
2600 Mission Bell Drive
San Pablo, CA 94806

Dominican College
1520 Grand Avenue
San Rafael, CA 94901

Feather River College
Highway 70 North
Quincy, CA 95971

Fullerton College
321 East Chapman Avenue
Fullerton, CA 92634

Hartnell Community College
156 Homestead Avenue
Salinas, CA 93901

Holy Names College
3500 Mountain Boulevard
Oakland, CA 94619-9989

Opportunities for Credit

Long Beach City College
4901 East Carson Street
Long Beach, CA   90808

Los Angeles Harbor College
1111 Figueroa Place
Wilmington, CA   90744-2397

Los Angeles Pierce College
6201 Winnetka Avenue
Woodland Hills, CA   91371

Marymount Palos Verdes
  College
30800 Palos Verdes Drive East
Rancho Palos Verdes, CA 90274

Merced College
3600 M Street
Merced, CA   95340

Modesto Junior College
College Avenue
Modesto, CA   95350-9977

Moorpark College
7075 Campus Road
Moorpark, CA   93021

Mount St. Mary's College
12001 Chalon Road
Los Angeles, CA 90049

Mount San Antonio College
1100 North Grand Avenue
Walnut, CA   91789

Mount San Jacinto College
1499 North State Street
San Jacinto, CA   92383

National University
4141 Camino Del Rio South
San Diego, CA   92108

New College of California
777 Valencia Street
San Francisco, CA   94110

Orange Coast College
P.O. Box 5005
Costa Mesa, CA   92628-0120

Palomar College
1140 West Mission
San Marcos, CA   92069-1487

Sacramento City College
3835 Freeport Boulevard
Sacramento,CA   95822

Saint Mary's College
P.O. Box 785
Moraga, CA   94575

San Bernardino Valley
  College
701 South Mt. Vernon Avenue
San Bernardino, CA   92410

San Diego Mesa College
7250 Mesa College Drive
San Diego, CA   92111-4998

San Diego Miramar College
10440 Black Mountain Road
San Diego, CA   92126

San Francisco State
  University
1600 Holloway Avenue
San Francisco, CA   94132

San Joaquin Delta College
5151 Pacific Avenue
Stockton, CA   95207

Santa Ana College
17th at Bristol
Santa Ana, CA   92706

Sierra College
5000 Rocklin Road
Rocklin, CA   95677

University of California,
  Santa Barbara
Santa Barbara, CA   93106

University of LaVerne
1950 Third Street
LaVerne, CA   91750

University of the Pacific
3601 Pacific Avenue
Stockton, CA   95211

CALIFORNIA (cont.)

University of Redlands
1200 East Colton Avenue
Redlands, CA 92374-3755

University of San Francisco
2130 Fulton Street
San Francisco, CA 94117-1080

West Coast Christian College
6901 North Maple Avenue
Fresno, CA 93710-4599

Whittier College
13406 East Phila P.O. Box 634
Whittier, CA 90608

Woodbury University
1027 Wilshire Boulevard
Los Angeles, CA 90017

Yuba College
2088 North Beale Road
Marysville, CA 95901

COLORADO

Adams State College
Alamosa, CO 81102

Aims Community College
P.O. Box 69
Greeley, CO 80632

Arapahoe Community College
5900 South Santa Fe Drive
Littleton, CO 80120-9988

Colorado College
Colorado Springs, CO 80903

Colorado Mountain College
P.O. Box 10001
Glenwood Springs, CO 81602

Colorado School of Mines
Golden, CO 80401

Colorado State University
Fort Collins, CO 80523

Fort Lewis College
Durango, CO 81301

Front Range Community
College
3645 West 112th Avenue
Westminster, CO 80030-2199

Iliff School of Theology
2201 South University
Boulevard
Denver, CO 80210

Loretto Heights College
3001 South Federal Boulevard
Denver, CO 80236

Metropolitan State College
1006 11th Street
Denver, CO 80204

Pueblo Community College
900 West Orman Avenue
Pueblo, CO 81004

Red Rocks Community College
12600 West Sixth Avenue
Golden, CO 80401

Regis College
3539 West 50th Parkway
Denver, CO 80221

Rockmont College
180 South Garrison
Lakewood, CO 80226

University of Colorado,
School of Medicine
4200 East 9th Avenue
Denver, CO 80262

University of Northern
Colorado
Greeley, CO 80639

University of Southern
Colorado
2200 N Bonforte Boulevard
Pueblo, CO 81001

CONNECTICUT

Albertus Magnus College
700 Prospect Street
New Haven, CT 06511

Briarwood College
2279 Mount Vernon Road
Southington, CT   06489

Fairfield University
Fairfield, CT   06430

Greater Hartford Community
  College
61 Woodland Street
Hartford, CT   06105

Housatonic Community College
510 Barnum Avenue
Bridgeport, CT   06608

Middlesex Community College
100 Training Hill Road
Middletown, CT   06457

Mitchell College
437 Pequot Avenue
New London, CT   06320

Mohegan Community College
Mahan Drive
Norwich, CT   06360

Northwestern Connecticut
  Community College
Park Place East
Winsted, CT   06098

Norwalk Community College
333 Wilson Avenue
Norwalk, CT   06854

Quinebaug Valley Community
  College
Maple Street P.O. Box 59
Danielson,CT   06239

Quinnipiac College
Mount Carmel Avenue
Hamden, CT   06518

Sacred Heart University
P.O. Box 6460
Bridgeport, CT   06606-0460

Saint Alphonsus College
1762 Mapleton Avenue
Suffield, CT   06078

Saint Joseph College
1678 Asylum Avenue
West Hartford, CT   06117

South Central Community
  College
60 Sargent Drive
New Haven, CT   06511

Tunxis Community College
Routes 6 and 177
Farmington, CT   06032

United States Coast Guard
  Academy
New London, CT   06320

University of Hartford
200 Bloomfield Avenue
West Hartford, CT 06117-0395

Western Connecticut State
  University
181 White Street
Danbury, CT   06810

DELAWARE
Delaware State College
1200 North Dupont Highway
Dover, DE   19901

University of Delaware
Newark, DE 19716

DISTRICT OF COLUMBIA
American University
4400 Massachusetts Avenue NW
Washington, DC   20016

Gallaudet College
800 Florida Avenue NE
Washington, DC   20002

Howard University
2400 Sixth Street NW
Washintgon, DC   20059

Mount Vernon College
2100 Foxhall Road NW
Washington, DC   20007

Southeastern University
501 Eye Street SW
Washington, DC   20024

DISTRICT OF COLUMBIA (cont.)
Trinity College
125 Michigan Avenue NE
Washington, DC 20017

FLORIDA
Barry University
11300 NE Second Avenue
Miami, FL 33161

Bethune Cookman College
640 Second Avenue
Daytona Beach, FL 32015

Brevard Community College
Clearlake Road
Cocoa, FL 32922

Broward Community College
7200 Hollywood Boulevard
Pembroke Pines, FL 33024

Daytona Beach Community
  College
P.O. Box 1111
Daytona Beach, FL 32015

Eckerd College
P.O. Box 12560
St. Petersburg, FL 33733

Edison Community College
8099 College Parkway SW
Fort Myers, FL 33907-9990

Embry-Riddle Aeronautical
  University
Star Route Box 540
Bunnell, FL 32010

Flagler College
P.O. Box 1027
St. Augustine, FL 32085-1027

Florida Junior College
501 West State Street
Jacksonville, FL 32202

Florida Keys Community
  College
Key West, FL 33040

Gulf Coast Community College
5230 West Highway 98
Panama City, FL 32401

Hillsborough Community
  College
P.O. Box 22127
Tampa, FL 33630

Lake Sumter Community
  College
5900 U S 441 South
Leesburg, FL 32748

Luther Rice Bible College &
  Seminary
1050 Hendricks Avenue
Jacksonville, FL 32207

Miami-Dade Community College
11011 SW 104th Street
Miami, FL 33176

National Education Center,
  Tampa Technical Institute
3920 East Hillsborough
  Avenue
Tampa, FL 33610

Nova College
3301 College Avenue
Fort Lauderdale, FL 33314

Rollins College
Winter Park, FL 32789-4499

Saint Leo College
State Road 52
Saint Leo, FL 33574

Saint Petersburg Junior
  College
P.O. Box 13489
St. Petersburg, FL 33733

Saint Thomas University
16400 NW 32nd Avenue
Miami, FL 33054

Southeastern College
1000 Longfellow Boulevard
Lakeland, FL 33801

Opportunities for Credit

University of Central Florida
P.O. Box 25000
Orlando, FL 32816

University of Miami
University Station
Coral Gables, FL 33124

University of South Florida
4202 Fowler Avenue
Tampa, FL 33620

University of Tampa
401 West Kennedy Boulevard
Tampa, FL 33606-1490

University of West Florida
Pensacola, FL 32514-0101

Valencia Community College
P.O. Box 3028
Orlando, FL 32802

Warner Southern College
5301 U S Highway 27 South
Lake Wales, FL 33853

GEORGIA
Andrew College
College Street
Cuthbert, GA 31740

Armstrong State College
11935 Abercorn Street
Savannah, GA 31419-1997

Atlanta Christian College
2605 Ben Hill Road
East Point, GA 30344-9989

Augusta College
2500 Walton Way
Augusta, GA 30910

Berry College
Mount Berry, GA 30149

Brunswick Junior College
Altama at Fourth Street
Brunswick, GA 31523

Clayton Junior College
P.O Box 285 5900 Lee Street
Morrow, GA 30260

Dalton Junior College
Dalton, GA 30720

Dekalb Community College
955 North Indian Creek Drive
Clarkston, GA 30021

Fort Valley State College
805 State College Drive
Fort Valley, GA 31030

Georgia College
Milledgeville, GA 31061

Georgia Southern College
Statesboro, GA 30460-8033

Georgia State University
University Plaza
Atlanta, GA 30303

Macon Junior College
U S 80 and I-475
Macon, GA 31297-4899

Mercer University, Atlanta
3001 Mercer University Drive
Atlanta, GA 30341

Mercer University, Macon
1400 Coleman Avenue
Macon, GA 31207

Middle Georgia College
Cochran, GA 31014

Paine College
1235 15th Street
Augusta, GA 30910-2799

Piedmont College
Demorest, GA 30535

Reinhardt College
Waleska, GA 30183

Tift College
Tift College Drive
Forsyth, GA 31029-2318

Toccoa Falls College
Toccoa Falls, GA 30598-0068

GEORGIA (cont.)
  Wesleyan College
  4760 Forsyth Road
  Macon, GA 31297-4299

HAWAII
  Brigham Young University,
  Hawaii Campus
  55-220 Kulanui Street
  Laie Oahu, HI 96762

  Chaminade University of
  Honolulu
  3140 Waialae Avenue
  Honolulu, HI 96816-1578

  Hawaii Loa College
  45-045 Kamehameha Highway
  Kaneohe, HI 96744-5297

  Hawaii Pacific College
  1060 Bishop Street
  Honolulu, HI 96813

  Honolulu Community College
  874 Dillingham Boulevard
  Honolulu, HI 96817

  Kapiolani Community College
  Pensacola Street
  Honolulu, HI 96814-2859

IDAHO
  Boise State University
  1910 University Drive
  Boise, ID 83725

  Idaho State University
  Pocatello, ID 83209-0009

  Lewis-Clark State College
  8th Avenue & 6th Street
  Lewiston, ID 83501

  North Idaho College
  1000 West Garden Avenue
  Coeur D'alene, ID 83814

ILLINOIS
  American Conservatory of
  Music
  116 South Michigan Avenue
  Chicago, IL 60603

Aurora College
347 South Gladstone Avenue
Aurora, IL 60507

Belleville Area College
2500 Carlyle Road
Belleville, IL 62221

Blackburn College
Carlinville, IL 62626

Black Hawk College, East
  Campus
Box 489
Kewanee, IL 61443

Chicago State University
95th Street at King Drive
Chicago, IL 60628

City Colleges of Chicago
30 East Lake Street
Chicago, IL 60601-2495

College of DuPage
22nd Street & Lambert Road
Glen Ellyn, IL 60137

College of Saint Francis
500 North Wilcox Street
Joliet, IL 60435

Columbia College
600 South Michigan Avenue
Chicago, IL 60605

De Paul University, School
  for New Learning
23 East Jackson Boulevard
Chicago, IL 60604-2287

Eastern Illinois University
Charleston, IL 61920

Frontier Community College
Rural Route #1
Fairfield, IL 62837

Garrett-Evangelical
  Theological Seminary
2121 Sheridan Road
Evanston, IL 60201

Opportunities for Credit

Governors State University
Park Forest South, IL   60466

Illinois Benedictine College
5700 College Road
Lisle, IL   60532-0900

Illinois Central College
East Peoria, IL   61635

Illinois College
Jacksonville, IL   62650-2299

Illinois State University
Normal, IL   61761

Illinois Valley Community
 College
2578 East 350th Road
Oglesby, IL   61348-1099

John Wood Community College
150 South 48th Street
Quincy, IL   62301-1498

Joliet Junior College
1216 Houbolt Avenue
Joliet, IL   60436-9352

Kaskaskia College
Shattuc Road
Centralia, IL   62801

Kishwaukee College
Route 38 & Malta Road
Malta, IL   60150

Lake Land College
South Route 45
Mattoon, IL   61938

Lincoln College
300 Keokuk Street
Lincoln, IL   62656

McHenry County College
Route 14 & Lucas Road
Crystal Lake, IL   60014

McKendree College
701 College Road
Lebanon, IL   62254-9990

Midstate College
244 S W Jefferson
Peoria, IL   61602

Moraine Valley Community
 College
10900 South 88th Avenue
Palos Hills, IL   60465-0937

Morton College
3801 South Central Avenue
Cicero, IL   60650

National College of
 Education, Evanston
2840 Sheridan Road
Evanston, IL   60201

National College of
 Education, Lombard
2 South 361 Glen Park Road
Lombard, IL   60148

Northeastern Illinois
 University
5500 North St. Louis Avenue
Chicago, IL   60625-4699

Northern Illinois University
De Kalb, IL   60115

Olivet Nazarene College
Kankakee, IL   60901

Prairie State College
P.O. Box 487
Chicago Heights, IL   60411

Richland Community College
2425 Federal Drive
Decatur,IL   62526

Rock Valley College
3301 North Mulford Road
Rockford, IL   61111

Roosevelt University
430 South Michigan Avenue
Chicago, IL   60605-1394

Rush University
600 South Paulina Street
Chicago, IL   60612

ILLINOIS (cont.)
Saint Xavier College
3700 West 103rd Street
Chicago, IL 60655

Sangamon State University
Springfield, IL 62708

Sauk Valley College
R F D No 5
Dixon, IL 61021

Sherwood Conservatory of
Music
1014 South Michigan Avenue
Chicago, IL 60605

Southeastern Illinois College
Route 4
Harrisburg, IL 62946

Spertus College of Judaica
618 South Michigan Avenue
Chicago, IL 60605

Spoon River College
Rural Route #1
Canton, IL 61520

Thornton Community College
15800 South State Street
South Holland, IL 60473

Trinity Christian College
6601 West College Drive
Palos Heights, IL 60463

Triton College
2000 5th Avenue
River Grove, IL 60171

University of Illinois,
Urbana-Champaign
Urbana, IL 61801

Wabash Valley College
2200 College Drive
Mount Carmel, IL 62863

Waubonsee Community College
State Route 47 at Harter Road
Sugar Grove, IL 60554

Western Illinois University
Adams Street
Macomb, IL 61455-1396

Wilbur Wright College
3400 North Austin Avenue
Chicago, IL 60634

INDIANA
Anderson College
Anderson, IN 46012-3462

Associated Mennonite
Biblical Seminaries
3003 Benham Avenue
Elkhart, IN 46517

Ball State University
Muncie, IN 47306

Bethel College
1001 West McKinley Avenue
Mishawaka, IN 46545-5591

Butler University
4600 Sunset Avenue
Indianapolis, IN 46208

Calumet College
2400 New York Avenue
Whiting, IN 46394

DePauw University
Greencastle, IN 46135

Franklin College
501 East Monroe Street
Franklin, IN 46131-2598

Goshen College
Goshen, IN 46526-4798

Grace College
200 Seminary Drive
Winona Lake, IN 46590

Huntington College
2303 College Avenue
Huntington, IN 46750-9986

Indiana State University,
Evansville
8600 University Boulevard
Evansville, IN 47712

Opportunities for Credit

Indiana State University,
  Terre Haute
217 North 6th Street
Terre Haute, IN 47809

Indiana University,
  Bloomington
Bryan Hall
Bloomington, IN 47405

Indiana University, Southeast
4201 Grant Line Road
New Albany, IN 47150

Indiana University-Purdue
  University, Indianapolis
355 North Lansing
Indianapolis, IN 46202

Indiana Vocational Technical
  College, Central Indiana
One West 26th Street,
  P.O. Box 1763
Indianapolis, IN 46206

Indiana Vocational Technical
  College, Eastcentral
4100 Cowan Road Box 3100
Muncie, IN 47302

Indiana Vocational Technical
  College, Kokomo
1815 East Morgan Street
Kokomo, IN 46901

Indiana Vocational Technical
  College, Lafayette
3208 Ross Road Box 6299
Lafayette, IN 47903

Indiana Vocational Technical
  College, Northcentral
1534 West Sample Street
South Bend, IN 46619

Indiana Vocational Technical
  College, Northeast
3800 North Anthony Boulevard
Fort Wayne, IN 46805

Indiana Vocational Technical
  College, Southwest
3501 North 1st Avenue
Evansville, IN 47710

Indiana Vocational Technical
  College, Wabash Valley
7377 Dixie Bee Road
Terre Haute, IN 47802

Indiana Vocational Technical
  College, Whitewater
2325 Chester Boulevard
Richmond, IN 47374

Manchester College
North Manchester, IN 46962

Marian College
3200 Cold Spring Road
Indianapolis, IN 46222

Martin Center College
3553 North College Avenue
Indianapolis, IN 46205

Oakland City College
Lucretia Street
Oakland City, IN 47660-1099

Saint Mary-of-the-Woods
  College
Saint Mary-of-the-Woods, IN
  47876

Saint Meinrad College
Saint Meinrad, IN 47577

Tri-State University
South Darling Street
Angola, IN 46703-0307

Vincennes University
1002 North First Street
Vincennes, IN 47591-9986

IOWA
Briar Cliff College
3303 Rebecca Street
Sioux City, IA 51104

Clarke College
1550 Clarke Drive
Dubuque, IA 52001-9983

Eastern Iowa Community
  College
2804 Eastern Avenue
Davenport, IA 52803

Opportunities for Credit

IOWA (cont.)
Faith Baptist Bible College
1900 NW 4th Street
Ankeny, IA 50021-2198

Grand View College
1200 Grand View Avenue
Des Moines, IA 50316-1599

Indian Hills Community
  College
Grandview & North Elm
Ottumwa, IA 52501

Iowa Lakes Community College
19 South 7th Street
Estherville, IA 51334

Iowa State University
Ames, Iowa 50011

Marshalltown Community
  College
3700 South Center Street
Marshalltown, IA 50158

Marycrest College
1607 West 12th Street
Davenport, IA 52804

Mount Mercy College
1330 Elmhurst Drive N E
Cedar Rapids, IA 52402

Mount Saint Clare College
400 North Bluff Boulevard
Clinton, IA 52732

Palmer College of
  Chiropractic
1000 Brady Street
Davenport, IA 52803

Saint Ambrose College
518 West Locust Street
Davenport, IA 52803

Simpson College
Indianola, IA 50125-1299

Southeastern Community
  College
Drawer F Highway 406
West Burlington, IA 52655

University of Dubuque
2000 University Avenue
Dubuque, IA 52001

University of Northern Iowa
1222 West 27th Street
Cedar Falls, IA 50614

Waldorf College
Forest City, IA 50436

Wartburg College
222 9th Street N W
Waverly, IA 50677

Westmar College
Le Mars, IA 51031

KANSAS
Allen County Community
  College
1801 North Cottonwood
Iola, KS 66749

Cloud County Community
  College
2221 Campus Drive
Concordia, KS 66901-1002

Cowley County Community
  College
125 South Second
Arkansas City, KS 67005

Donnelly College
608 North 18th Street
Kansas City, KS 66102

Fort Hays State University
600 Park Street
Hays, KS 67601-4099

Hesston College
Hesston, KS 67062

Independence Community
  College
Brookside Drive & College
  Avenue
Independence, KS 67301-9998

Opportunities for Credit

Johnson County Community
  College
12345 College at Quivira
Overland Park, KS 66210-1299

Kansas City Kansas Community
  College
7250 State Avenue
Kansas City, Kansas 66112

Kansas Newman College
3100 McCormick Avenue
Wichita, KS 67213

Kansas State University
Manhattan, KS 66506

Manhattan Christian College
1407 Anderson
Manhattan, KS 66502

Mid-America Nazarene College
2030 College Way
Olathe, KS 66061-1776

Ottawa Univeristy, Kansas
  City
10865 Grand View, Building 20
Overland Park, KS 66210

Ottawa University, Ottawa
10th at Cedar
Ottawa, KS 66067

Pittsburg State University
Pittsburg, KS 66762

Seward County Community
  College
Box 1137
Liberal, KS 67901

Southwestern College
Winfield, KS 67156

Washburn University
17th and College
Topeka, KS 66621

Wichita State University
Wichita, KS 67208

KENTUCKY
Ashland Community College
1400 College Drive
Ashland, KY 41101

Brescia College
120 West Seventh Street
Owensboro, KY 42301

Centre College
Danville, KY 40422

Eastern Kentucky University
Richmond, KY 40475-0931

Kentucky State University
East Main Street
Frankfort, KY 40601

Kentucky Wesleyan College
Owensboro, KY 42301

Lindsey Wilson College
210 Lindsey Wilson Street
Columbia, KY 42728

Northern Kentucky University
University Drive
Highland Heights, KY 41076

Paducah Community College
P.O. Box 7380
Paducah, KY 42001-7380

Pikeville College
Sycamore Street
Pikeville, KY 41501-1194

Saint Catharine College
Saint Catharine, KY 40061

Southern Baptist Theological
  Seminary
2825 Lexington Road
Louisville, KY 40280

Thomas More College
Fort Mitchell, KY 41017

Union College
College Street
Barbourville, KY 40906

Opportunities for Credit

KENTUCKY (cont.)
University of Louisville
South Third Street
Louisville, KY 40292

Western Kentucky University
Bowling Green, KY 42101

LOUISIANA
Centenary College of
Louisiana
P.O. Box 4188
Shreveport, LA 71134-0188

Louisiana State University
and Agricultural and
Mechanical College
Baton Rouge, LA 70803

Louisiana State University,
Alexandria
Alexandria, LA 71302

Louisiana State University,
Eunice
P.O. Box 1129
Eunice, LA 70535

Louisiana State University,
Shreveport
8515 Youree Drive
Shreveport, LA 71115

McNeese State University
4100 Ryan Street
Lake Charles, LA 70609

Nicholls State University
University Station
Thibodaux, LA 70310

Northwestern State University
Natchitoches, LA 71497

Our Lady of Holy Cross
College
4123 Woodland Drive
New Orleans, LA 70114

Southeastern Louisiana
University
100 West Dakota
Hammond, LA 70402

Southern University and
Agricultural and Mechanical
College, Baton Rouge
Baton Rouge, LA 70813

Southern University,
New Orleans
6400 Press Drive
New Orleans, LA 70126

Xavier University of
Louisiana
Palmetto & Pine Streets
New Orleans, LA 70125

MAINE
Andover College
901 Washington Avenue
Portland, ME 04103

Central Maine Vocational-
Technical Institute
1250 Turner Street
Auburn, ME 04210

Eastern Maine Vocational-
Technical Institute
354 Hogan Road
Bangor, ME 04401

Portland School of Art
97 Spring Street
Portland, ME 04101

Saint Joseph's College
North Windham, ME 04062

Southern Maine Vocational-
Technical Institute
Fort Road
South Portland, ME 04106

University of Maine, Augusta
University Heights
Augusta, ME 04330

University of Maine, Machias
Machias, ME 04654

Univeristy of Maine, Orono
Orono, ME 04469

Opportunities for Credit

University of Southern Maine
96 Falmouth Street
Portland, ME   04103

MARYLAND
Baltimore Hebrew College
5800 Park Heights Avenue
Baltimore, MD   21215

Bowie State College
Jericho Park Road
Bowie, MD   20715

Capitol Institute of
 Technology
11301 Springfield Road
Laurel, MD   20708

Catonsville Community
 College
800 South Rolling Road
Baltimore, MD   21228

Cecil Community College
1000 North East Road
North East, MD   21901-1999

Chesapeake College
Wye Mills, MD   21679

College of Notre Dame of
 Maryland
4701 North Charles Street
Baltimore, MD   21210

Columbia Union College
7600 Flower Avenue
Takoma Park, MD   20912

Dundalk Community College
7200 Sollers Point Road
Baltimore, MD   21222-4692

Frostburg State College
Frostburg, MD   21532

Garrett Community College
Mosser Road
McHenry, MD   21541

Goucher College
Towson, MD   21204

Hagerstown Junior College
751 Robinwood Drive
Hagerstown, MD   21740-6590

Harford Community College
401 Thomas Run Road
Bel Air, MD   21014

Hood College
Rosemont Avenue
Frederick, MD   21701

Howard Community College
Little Patuxent Parkway
Columbia, MD   21044-3197

Maryland Institute College
 of Art
1300 West Mount Royal Avenue
Baltimore, MD   21217

Montgomery College
51 Mannakee Street
Rockville, MD   20850

Mount Saint Mary's College
Emmitsburg, MD   21727

Prince George's Community
 College
301 Largo Road
Largo, MD   20772

Saint Mary's College of
 Maryland
Saint Mary's City, MD   20686

Salisbury State College
Salisbury, MD   21801

United States Naval Academy
Annapolis, MD   21402

University of Baltimore
Charles at Mount Royal
Baltimore, MD   21201

University of Maryland,
 College Park
College Park, MD   20742

Opportunities for Credit

MARYLAND (cont.)
University of Maryland,
University College
University Boulevard at
Adelphi Road
College Park, MD   20742

Villa Julie College
Green Spring Valley Road
Stevenson, MD   21153

Washington College
Chestertown, MD   21620

Western Maryland College
Westminster, MD   21157-4390

MASSACHUSETTS
American International
College
1000 State Street
Springfield, MA   01109

Assumption College
500 Salisbury Street
Worcester, MA   01609-1296

Atlantic Union College
South Lancaster, MA   01561

Berkshire Christian College
Lenox, MA   01240

Berkshire Community College
West Street
Pittsfield, MA   01201

Bradford College
320 South Main Street
Bradford, MA   01830

Brandeis University
415 South Street
Waltham, MA   02154

Bridgewater State College
Bridegwater, MA   02324

Bristol Community College
777 Elsbree Street
Fall River, MA   02720-7395

Central New England College
of Technology
678 Main Street
Worcester, MA   01610

Clark University
950 Main Street
Worcester, MA   01610

College of Our Lady of the
Elms
291 Springfield Street
Chicopee, MA   01013-2839

Curry College
1071 Blue Hill Avenue
Milton, MA   02186

Fitchburg State College
160 Pearl Street
Fitchburg, MA   01420

Greenfield Community College
1 College Drive
Greenfield, MA   01301

Hampshire College
Amherst, MA   01002

Hellenic College
50 Goddard Avenue
Brookline, MA   02146

Laboure College
2120 Dorchester Avenue
Boston, MA   02124-5698

Massachusetts College of Art
621 Huntington Avenue
Boston, MA   02115

Massachusetts College of
Pharmacy and Allied Health
Services
179 Longwood Avenue
Boston, MA   02115

Middlesex Community College
Springs Road
Bedford, MA   01730

Mount Ida College
777 Dedham Street
Newton Centre, MA   02159

List of Institutions

Opportunities for Credit

Mount Wachusett Community
  College
444 Green Street
Gardner, MA 01440

New England College of
  Optometry
424 Beacon Street
Boston, MA 02115

North Adams State College
Church Street
North Adams, MA 01247

North Shore Community
  College
3 Essex Street
Beverly, MA 01915

Pine Manor College
400 Heath Street
Chestnut Hill, MA 02167

Salem State College
352 Lafayette Street
Salem, MA 01970

Simmons College
300 The Fenway
Boston, MA 02115

Simon's Rock of Bard College
Great Barrington, MA 01230

Springfield Technical
  Community College
Armory Square
Springfield, MA 01105

University of Massachusetts,
  Amherst
Amherst, MA 01003

University of Massachusetts,
  Boston
Harbor Campus
Boston, MA 02125

Wentworth Institute of
  Technology
550 Huntington Avenue
Boston, MA 02115

Western New England College
1215 Wilbraham Road
Springfield, MA 01119-2684

Wheelock College
200 The Riverway
Boston, MA 02215

Worcester State College
486 Chandler Street
Worcester, MA 01602-2597

MICHIGAN
Adrian College
Adrian, MI 49221-2575

Andrews University
Berrien Springs, MI 49104

Aquinas College
1607 Robinson Road SE
Grand Rapids, MI 49506

Baker Junior College
1110 Eldon Baker Drive
Flint, MI 48507-1986

Central Michigan University
Mount Pleasant, MI 48859

Concordia College
4090 Geddes Road
Ann Arbor, MI 48105-2797

Delta College
University Center, MI 48710

Ferris State College
Big Rapids, MI 49307

Grand Rapids Baptist College
1001 East Beltline Avenue NE
Grand Rapids, MI 49505

Grand Rapids Junior College
143 Bostwick Avenue NE
Grand Rapids, MI 49503

Jackson Community College
2111 Emmons Road
Jackson, MI 49201

MICHIGAN (cont.)
Kalamazoo College
1200 Academy Street
Kalamazoo, MI 49007

Kalamazoo Valley Community
  College
6767 West O Avenue
Kalamazoo, MI 49009

Kirtland Community College
Route #4 Box 59-A
Roscommon, MI 48653-9721

Lake Superior State College
Sault Sainte Marie, MI
  49783-9981

Madonna College
36600 Schoolcraft Road
Livonia, MI 48150-1173

Marygrove College
8425 West McNichols Road
Detroit, MI 48221-2599

Michigan Christian College
800 West Avon Road
Rochester, MI 48063

Michigan State University
50 Kellogg Center
East Lansing, MI 48824-1022

Monroe County Community
  College
1555 S Raisinville Road
Monroe, MI 48161

Muskegon Community College
221 South Quarterline Road
Muskegon, MI 49442

Nazareth College
Nazareth, MI 49074

Northwood Institute
3225 Cook Road
Midland, MI 48640

Oakland Community College
Box 812
Bloomfield Hills, MI 48013

Oakland University
Rochester, MI 48063

Sacred Heart Seminary
  College
2701 Chicago Boulevard
Detroit, MI 48206

Saint Clair County Community
  College
323 Erie Street
Port Huron, MI 48060

Southwestern Michigan
  College
Cherry Grove Road
Dowagiac, MI 49047

Spring Arbor College
106 Main Street
Spring Arbor, MI 49283

Suomi College
Hancock, MI 49930

University of Michigan
Ann Arbor, MI 48109

Wayne State University
Detroit, MI 48202

West Shore Community College
3000 North Stiles
Scottville, MI 49454-0277

Western Michigan University
Kalamazoo, MI 49008-3899

MINNESOTA
Anoka Ramsey Community
  College
11200 Mississippi River
  Boulevard NW
Coon Rapids, MN 55433

Arrowhead Community College
  Region, Vermilion Community
  College
1900 East Camp Street
Ely, MN 55731

Austin Community College
1600 8th Avenue NW
Austin, MN 55912

Opportunities for Credit

Bemidji State University
Bemidji, MN 56601

College of Saint Scholastica
1200 Kenwood Avenue
Duluth, MN 55811

College of Saint Teresa
Winona, MN 55987-0837

College of Saint Thomas
2115 Summit Avenue
Saint Paul, MN 55105

Concordia College,
 Saint Paul
Hamline and Marshall Avenue
Saint Paul, MN 55104

Dr. Martin Luther College
College Heights
New Ulm, MN 56073

Golden Valley Lutheran
 College
6125 Olson Highway
Minneapolis, MN 55422

Inver Hills Community
 College
8445 College Trail
Inver Grove Heights, MN
55075

Lakewood Community College
3401 Century Avenue
White Bear Lake, MN 55110

Mankato State University
South Road and Ellis Avenue
Mankato, MN 56001

Metropolitan State
 University
121 Metro Square
Saint Paul, MN 55101

Minneapolis Community
 College
1501 Hennepin Avenue
Minneapolis, MN 55403

Minnesota Bible College
920 Mayowood Road SW
Rochester, MN 55902

Moorhead State University
11th Street South
Moorhead, MN 56560-9980

North Hennepin Community
 College
7411 85th Avenue North
Brooklyn Park, MN 55445

Rochester Community College
Highway 14 East
Rochester, MN 55904

Saint Cloud State University
Saint Cloud, MN 56301

Saint Mary's College
Winona, MN 55987

University of Minnesota,
 Morris
Morris, MN 56267

University of Minnesota
 Technical College, Waseca
Waseca, MN 56093

Willmar Community College
Willmar, MN 56201

Worthington Community
 College
1450 Collegeway
Worthington, MN 56187

MISSISSIPPI
Alcorn State University
Lorman, MS 39096-9998

Millsaps College
Jackson, MS 39210-0001

Mississippi Gulf Coast
 Junior College
Perkinston, MS 39573

Reformed Theological
 Seminary
5422 Clinton Boulevard
Jackson, MS 39209

Opportunities for Credit

MISSISSIPPI (cont.)
University of Mississippi
University, MS 38677

Wesley College
Florence, MS 39073-0070

William Carey College
Hattiesburg, MS 39401

MISSOURI
Avila College
11901 Wornall Road
Kansas City, MO 64145-9990

Calvary Bible College
Kansas City, MO 64147

Central Missouri State
 University
Warrensburg, MO 64093

Columbia College
10th and Rogers
Columbia, MO 65216

Cottey College
1000 West Austin
Nevada, MO 64772-1000

Crowder College
Neosho, MO 64850

Culver-Stockton College
College Hill
Canton, MO 63435-9989

East Central College
P.O. Box 529
Union, MO 63084

Evangel College
1111 North Glenstone
Springfield, MO 65802

Fontbonne College
6800 Wydown Boulevard
Saint Louis, MO 63105

Hannibal-LaGrange College
Hannibal, MO 63401

Harris-Stowe State College
3026 Laclede Avenue
Saint Louis, MO 63103

Jefferson College
Hillsboro, 63050-1000

Kemper Military School and
 College
701 Third Street
Boonville, MO 65233

Lincoln University
820 Chestnut
Jefferson City, MO 65101

Lindenwood College
First Capitol and
 Kingshighway
Saint Charles, MO 63301

Longview Community College
500 Longview Road
Lee's Summit, MO 64063

Maple Woods Community
 College
2601 NE Barry Road
Kansas City, MO 64156-1299

Maryville College
13550 Conway Road
Saint Louis, MO 63141

Missouri Western State
 College
4525 Downs Drive
Saint Joseph, MO 64507-2294

Moberly Area Junior College
College and Rollins Streets
Moberly, MO 65270

Park College
Mackay Hall
Parkville, MO 64152

Saint Louis College of
 Pharmacy
4588 Parkview Place
Saint Louis, MO 63110

List of Institutions

Saint Louis Community College
5801 Wilson Avenue
Saint Louis, MO   63110

Saint Louis Community,
 Meramec
11333 Big Bend Boulevard
Kirkwood, MO   63122

Saint Louis University,
 Metropolitan College
221 North Grand Boulevard
Saint Louis, MO   63103

State Fair Community College
1900 Clarendon Road
Sedalia, MO   65301

Stephens College
Columbia, MO   65215-0001

University of Missouri,
 Columbia
Columbia, MO   65211

University of Missouri,
 Kansas City
5100 Rockhill Road
Kansas City, MO   64110

University of Missouri,
 Saint Louis
8001 Natural Bridge Road
Saint Louis, MO   63121

Webster University
470 East Lockwood
Saint Louis, MO   63119-3194

William Jewell College
Liberty, MO   64068

MONTANA
Carroll College
Helena, MT   59625

Dawson Community College
Box 421
Glendive, MT   59330

Eastern Montana College
1500 North 27th Street
Billings, MT   59101

Miles Community College
2715 Dickinson
Miles City, MT   59301

Rocky Mountain College
1511 Poly Drive
Billings, MT   59102-1796

NEBRASKA
Bellevue College
Bellevue, NE   68005-3098

Central Community College,
 Hastings
P.O. Box 1024
Hastings, NE   68901

Central Community College,
 Platte
P.O. Box 1027
Columbus, NE   68601

Central Technical Community
 College Area
P.O. Box C
Grand Island, NE   68802-0240

Chadron State College
10th and Main Streets
Chadron, NE   69337

College of Saint Mary
1901 South 72nd Street
Omaha, NE   68124

Dana College
Blair, NE   68008

Doane College
Crete, NE   68333

Hastings College
7th and Turner Avenue
Hastings, NE   68901

Mid-Plains Community
 College Area
416 North Jeffers
North Platte, NE   69101

Mid-Plains Community College
Route 4, Box 1
North Platte, NE   69101

Opportunities for Credit

NEBRASKA (cont.)
Nebraska Wesleyan University
5000 Saint Paul Street
Lincoln, NE   68504

Northeast Technical Community
  College
801 East Benjamin Avenue
P.O. Box 469
Norfolk, NE   68701

Peru State College
Peru, NE   68421

University of Nebraska,
  Lincoln
14th and R Streets
Lincoln, NE   68588

Wayne State College
Wayne, NE   68787

NEW HAMPSHIRE
Colby-Sawyer College
New London, NH   03257

Franklin Pierce College
Rindge, NH   03461

Keene State College
229 Main Street
Keene, NH   03401-4183

New Hampshire Technical
  Institute
Fan Road
Concord, NH   03301

New Hampshire Vocational-
  Technical College,
  Berlin
2020 Riverside Drive
Berlin, NH   03570-3799

New Hampshire Vocational-
  Technical College,
  Manchester
1066 Front Street
Manchester, NH   03102

New Hampshire Vocational-
  Technical College, Nashua
505 Amherst Street
Nashua, NH   03063-1092

Notre Dame College
2321 Elm Street
Manchester, NH   03104

Plymouth State College
Plymouth, NH   03264

School for Lifelong Learning
Dunlap Center
Durham, NH   03824-3545

NEW JERSEY
Brookdale Community College
Newman Springs Road
Lincroft, NJ   07738

Camden County College
P.O. Box 200
Blackwood, NJ   08012-0200

Centenary College
400 Jefferson Street
Hackettstown, NJ   07840

Cumberland County College
P.O. Box 517
Vineland NJ   08360-0517

Essex County College
303 University Avenue
Newark, NJ   07102

Georgian Court College
Lakewood, NJ   08701

Glassboro State College
Glassboro, NJ   08028

Gloucester County College
Tanyard Road-Deptford P.O.
Sewell, NJ   08080

Jersey City State College
2039 Kennedy Boulevard
Jersey City, NJ   07305-1597

Kean College of New Jersey
Morris Avenue
Union, NJ   07083

Mercer County Community
  College
1200 Old Trenton Road
Trenton, NJ   08690

Opportunities for Credit

Middlesex County College
Edison, NJ 08818

Monmouth College
Cedar and Norwood Avenues
West Long Branch, NJ 07764

New Brunswick Theological
  Seminary
17 Seminary Place
New Brunswick, NJ 08901

New Jersey Institute of
  Technology
323 High Street
Newark, NJ 07102

Passaic County Community
  College
College Boulevard
Paterson, NJ 07509

Ramapo College of New Jersey
505 Ramapo Valley Road
Mahwah, NJ 07430

Saint Peter's College
2641 Kennedy Boulevard
Jersey City, NJ 07306

Salem Community College
Penns Grove, NJ 08069-2799

Somerset County College
P.O. Box 3300
Somerville, NJ 08876-1265

Thomas A. Edison State
  College
101 West State Street
Trenton, NJ 08625

Trenton State College
CN 550 Hillwood Lakes
Trenton, NJ 08625

Union County College
1033 Springfield Avenue
Cranford, NJ 07016

Upsala College
East Orange, NJ 07019

William Paterson College
300 Pompton Road
Wayne, NJ 07470

NEW MEXICO
College of Santa Fe
St. Michael's Drive
Santa Fe, NM 87501

College of the Southwest
Lovington Highway
Hobbs, NM 88240

Eastern New Mexico
  University, Portales
Portales, NM 88130

Eastern New Mexico
  University, Roswell
P.O. Box 6000
Roswell, NM 88201

New Mexico Highlands
  University
Las Vegas, NM 87701

New Mexico State
  University, Alamogordo
Box 477
Alamogordo, NM 88310

San Juan College
4601 College Boulevard
Farmington NM 87401

Western New Mexico
  University
Silver City, NM 88061

NEW YORK
Academy of Aeronautics
La Guardia Airport
Flushing, NY 11371

Adelphi University,
  University College
Garden City, NY 11530

Adirondack Community College
Glens Falls, NY 12801

Opportunities for Credit

NEW YORK (cont.)

Albany College of Pharmacy
of Union University
106 New Scotland Avenue
Albany, NY   12208

Boricua College
3755 Broadway
New York, NY   10032

Broome Community College
P.O. Box 1017
Binghamton, NY   13902

Canisius College
2001 Main Street
Buffalo, NY   14208

Cayuga County Community
College
Franklin Street
Auburn, NY   13021

Christ the King Seminary
711 Knox Road   Box 160
East Aurora, NY   14052

City University of New York,
City College
Convent Avenue at 138th
Street
New York, NY   10031

Clinton Community College
Plattsburgh, NY   12901

Colgate University
Hamilton, NY   13346

College of Insurance
101 Murray Street
New York, NY   10007

College of New Rochelle,
School of New Resources
New Rochelle, NY   10801

Community College of the
Finger Lakes
Lincoln Hill
Canandaigua, NY   14424

Cooper Union
41 Cooper Square
New York, NY   10003

Corning Community College
Corning, NY   14830

Daeman College
4380 Main Street
Amherst, NY   14226

Dominican College of
Blauvelt
Western Highway
Orangeburg, NY   10962

Dowling College
Idle Hour Boulevard
Oakdale Long Island, NY
11769

D'Youville College
320 Porter Avenue
Buffalo, NY   14201

Elizabeth Seton College
1061 North Broadway
Yonkers, NY   10701

Elmira College
Park Place
Elmira, NY   14901-2099

Erie Community College,
City Campus
121 Ellicott Street
Buffalo, NY   14203

Erie Community College,
North
Main Street & Youngs Road
Buffalo, NY   14221

Erie Community College,
South
4140 Southwestern Boulevard
Orchard Park, NY   14127

Fashion Institute of
Technology
227 West 27th Street
New York, NY   10001

Opportunities for Credit

Fulton-Montgomery Community
  College
Route 67
Johnstown, NY 12095

Hartwick College
Oneonta, NY 13820

Herkimer County Community
  College
Reservoir Road
Herkimer, NY 13350

Houghton College
Houghton, NY 14744

Iona College
New Rochelle, NY 10801-1890

Ithaca College
Ithaca, NY 14850

Jamestown Community College
525 Falconer Street
Jamestown, NY 14701

Keuka College
Keuka Park, NY 14478-0098

Kingsborough Community
  College
2001 Oriental Boulevard
Brooklyn, NY 11235

Long Island University,
  Southampton
Montauk Highway
Southampton, NY 11968

Manhattanville College
Purchase, NY 10577

Marist College
82 North Road
Poughkeepsie, NY 12601

Marymount College
Tarrytown, NY 10591

Mater Dei College
Rural 2
Ogdensburg, NY 13669

Medaille College
18 Agassiz Circle
Buffalo, NY 14214

Mohawk Valley Community
  College
1101 Sherman Drive
Utica, NY 13501-5394

Molloy College
1000 Hempstead Avenue
Rockville Centre, NY 11570

Monroe Business Institute
29 East Fordham Road
Bronx, NY 10468

Mount Saint Mary College
Newburgh, NY 12550

Nassau Community College
Stewart Avenue
Garden City, NY 11530

Nazareth College of
  Rochester
4245 East Avenue
Rochester, NY 14610

New York University
70 Washington Square South
New York, NY 10012

Onondaga Community College
Onondaga Hill Road
Syracuse, NY 13215

Orange County Community
  College
115 South Street
Middletown, NY 10940

Pace University, New York
Pace Plaza
New York, NY 10038

Paul Smith's College
Paul Smiths, NY 12970

Pratt Institute
200 Willoughby Avenue
Brooklyn, NY 11205

Opportunities for Credit

NEW YORK (cont.)
Queensborough Community
  College
Bayside
New York, NY 11364

Rensselaer Polytechnic
  Institute
Troy, NY 12181

Roberts Wesleyan College
2301 Westside Drive
Rochester, NY 14624

Rockland Community College
145 College Road
Suffern, NY 10901

Saint Francis College
180 Remsen Street
Brooklyn, NY 11201

School of Visual Arts
209 East 23rd Street
New York, NY 10010

Siena College
Loudonville, NY 12211

Skidmore College, University
  Without Walls
Saratoga Springs, NY
  12866-0851

State University of New
  York, Agricultural &
  Technical College, Alfred
Alfred, NY 14802-1196

State University of New York
  Agricultural & Technical
  College, Canton
Canton, NY 13617

State University of New York
  Agricultural & Technical
  College, Delhi
Delhi, NY 13753-1190

State University of New York
  Agricultural & Technical
  College, Farmingdale
Melville Road
Farmingdale, NY 11735

SUNY, Brockport
Brockport, NY 14420

SUNY, Buffalo
1300 Elmwood Avenue
Buffalo, NY 14222

SUNY, Empire State College
2 Union Avenue
Saratoga Springs, NY 12866

SUNY, Fredonia
Fredonia, NY 14063

SUNY, Geneseo
Geneseo, NY 14454

SUNY, New Paltz
New Paltz, NY 12561

SUNY, Old Westbury
Box 210
Old Westbury, NY 11568

SUNY, Oneonta
Oneonta, NY 13820-1361

SUNY, Oswego
Oswego, NY 13126

SUNY, Purchase
Purchase, NY 10577

SUNY, Stony Brook
Stony Brook, NY 11794

Suffolk County Community
  College, Ammerman
533 College Road
Selden, NY 11784

Trocaire College
110 Red Jacket Parkway
Buffalo, NY 14220

Ulster County Community
  College
Stone Ridge, NY 12484

University of Rochester
Rochester, NY 14627

Opportunities for Credit

University of the State of
New York, Regents College
Degrees
Cultural Education Center
Albany, NY 12230

Utica College of Syracuse
University
Burrstone Road
Utica, NY 13502

NORTH CAROLINA
Belmont Abbey College
Belmont, NC 28012

Bladen Technical College
P.O. Box 266
Dublin, NC 28332-0266

Catawba College
Salisbury, NC 28144-2488

Central Piedmont Community
College
P.O. Box 35009
Charlotte, NC 28235

Coastal Carolina Community
College
444 Western Boulevard
Jacksonville, NC 28540-6877

Craven Community College
P.O. Box 885
New Bern, NC 28560

Davidson College
Davidson, NC 28036

East Carolina University
Greenvile, NC 27834

Edgecombe Technical College
2009 West Wilson
Tarboro, NC 27886

Elizabeth City State
University
Parkview Drive
Elizabeth City, NC 27909

Fayetteville Technical
Institute
P.O. Box 35236
Fayettville, NC 28303-0236

Forsyth Technical Institute
2100 Silas Creek Parkway
Winston-Salem, NC
27103-5197

Gardner-Webb College
Boiling Springs, NC 28017

Guilford Technical Community
College
P.O. Box 309
Jamestown, NC 27282

Halifax Community College
P.O. Box 809
Weldon, NC 27890

Haywood Technical College
Freedlander Drive
Clyde, NC 28721

Isothermal Community College
P.O. Box 804
Spindale, NC 28160-0804

James Sprunt Technical
College
P.O. Box 398
Kenansville, NC 28349-0398

Lenoir-Rhyne College
Hickory, NC 28603

Mayland Technical College
P.O. Box 547
Spruce Pine, NC 28777

Meredith College
Raleigh, NC 27607-5298

Mount Olive College
Mount Olive, NC 28365

North Carolina Central
University
Durham, NC 27707

NORTH CAROLINA (cont.)
Pfeiffer College, Charlotte
1416 East Morehead Street
Charlotte, NC 28204

Piedmont Technical College
P.O. Box 1197
Roxboro, NC 27573

Rowan Technical College
P.O. Box 1595
Salisbury, NC 28144

Sacred Heart College
414 North Main Street
Belmont, NC 28012

Saint Andrews Presbyterian
  College
Laurinburg, NC 28352

Salem College
Winston-Salem, NC 27108

Shaw University
118 East South Street
Raleigh, NC 27611

Southeastern Community
  College
P.O. Box 151
Whiteville, NC 28472-0151

Southwestern Technical
  College
275 Webster Road
Sylva, NC 28779

Surry Community College
South Main Street
Dobson, NC 27017-0304

University of North
  Carolina, Charlotte
UNCC Station
Charlotte, NC 28223

University of North
  Carolina, Greensboro
1000 Spring Garden Street
Greensboro, NC 27412-5001

University of North
  Carolina, Wilmington
601 South College Road
Wilmington, NC 28403-3297

Warren Wilson College
701 Warren Wilson Road
Swannanoa, NC 28778-2099

Wayne Community College
Caller Box 8002
Goldsboro, NC 27533-8002

Western Carolina University
Cullowhee, NC 28723

Western Piedmont Community
  College
1001 Burkemont Avenue
Morgantown, NC 28655-9978

Wilson County Technical
  Institute
902 Herring Avenue
Wilson, NC 27893-4305

NORTH DAKOTA
Dickinson State College
Dickinson, ND 58601-4896

Lake Region Community
  College
College Drive
Devils Lake, ND 58301

Mary College
Apple Creek Road
Bismarck, ND 58501

Trinity Bible College
50 6th Avenue South
Ellendale, ND 58436

Valley City State College
College Street
Valley City, ND 58072

OHIO
Antioch University
Yellow Springs, OH 45387

Ashland College
401 College Avenue
Ashland, OH 44805

Opportunities for Credit

Baldwin-Wallace College
275 Eastland Road
Berea, OH 44017

Bowling Green State
University, Bowling Green
Bowling Green, OH 43403

Bowling Green State
University, Firelands
College
901 Rye Beach Road
Huron, OH 44839

Capital University
East Main Sreet
Columbus, OH 43209

Chatfield Colege
Saint Martin, OH 45118

Cincinnati Technical College
3520 Central Parkway
Cincinnati, OH 45223

Clark Technical College
570 East Leffel Lane
Springfield, OH 45505

Cleveland Institute of Music
11021 East Boulevard
Cleveland, OH 44106

College of Mount Saint
Joseph
Mount Saint Joseph, OH
45051

Columbus Technical Institute
P.O. Box 1609
550 East Spring Street
Columbus, OH 43216-9965

Cuyahoga Community College
700 Carnegie Avenue
Cleveland, OH 44115

Cuyahoga Community College,
Western Campus
11000 West Pleasant Valley
Road
Parma, OH 44130

Defiance College
Defiance, OH 43512

Denison University
Granville, OH 43023

Findlay College
1000 North Main Street
Findlay, OH 45840

Franklin University
201 South Grant Avenue
Columbus, OH 43215-5399

Heidelberg Colege
310 East Market Street
Tiffin, OH 44883

Hiram College
Hiram, OH 44234

Hocking Technical College
Route 1
Nelsonville, OH 45764-9704

Kent State University,
Ashtabula
3325 West 13th Street
Ashtabula, OH 44004

Kent State University,
Tuscarawas Campus
University Drive NE
New Philadelphia, OH 44663

Lake Erie College
391 West Washington Street
Painesville, OH 44077

Lakeland Community College
Mentor, OH 44060

Lima Technical College
4240 Campus Drive
Lima, OH 45804

Lorain County Community
College
1005 North Abbe Road
Elyria, OH 44035

Lourdes College
6832 Convent Boulevard
Sylvania, OH 43560

Opportunities for Credit

OHIO (cont.)
Malone College
515 25th Street NW
Canton, OH 44709-3897

Miami University, Hamilton
1601 Peck Boulevard
Hamilton, OH 45011

Miami University, Oxford
Oxford, OH 45056

Mount Union College
1972 Clark Avenue
Alliance, OH 44601

Mount Vernon Nazarene
  College
800 Martinsburg Road
Mount Vernon, OH 43050

Muskingum Area Technical
  College
1555 Newark Road
Zanesville, OH 43701

Muskingum College
New Concord, OH 43762-1199

North Central Technical
  College
2441 Kenwood Circle
Mansfield, OH 44906

Notre Dame College
4545 College Road
Cleveland, OH 44121

Ohio Dominican College
1216 Sunbury Road
Columbus, OH 43219

Ohio State University,
  Columbus
Admissions Office, Third
  Floor, Lincon Tower
1800 Cannon Drive
Columbus, OH 43210-1358

Ohio State University, Lima
4240 Campus Drive
Lima, OH 45804

Ohio State University,
  Mansfield
1680 University Drive
Mansfield, OH 44906

Ohio State University,
  Marion
1465 Mount Vernon Avenue
Marion, OH 43302-5695

Ohio University, Athens
Athens, OH 45701

Otterbein College
Westerville, OH 43081

Owens Technical College
Oregon Road
Toledo, OH 43699

Shawnee State Community
  College
940 Second Street
Portsmouth, OH 45662

Sinclair Community College
444 West Third Street
Dayton, OH 45402-1460

Southern State Community
  College
200 Hobart Drive
Hillsboro, OH 45133

Stark Technical College
6200 Frank Avenue NW
Canton, OH 44720

Terra Technical College
1120 Cedar Street
Fremont, OH 43420

Union for Experimenting
  Colleges and Universities
632 Vine Street Suite 1010
Cincinnati, OH 45202-2407

University of Cincinnati,
  Cincinnati
Cincinnati, OH 45221

University of Cincinnati,
  Clermont College
College Drive
Batavia, OH   45103-1785

University of Steubenville
Franciscan Way
Steubenville, OH   43952

University of Toledo
2801 West Bancroft Street
Toledo, OH   43606

University of Toledo,
  Community & Technical
  College
Toledo, OH   43606

Urbana University
College Way
Urbana, OH   43078-9988

Ursuline College
2550 Lander Road
Cleveland, OH   44124

Walsh College
2020 Eastern Street NW
Canton, OH   44720

Washington Technical College
Route 2
Marietta, OH   45750

Wilberforce University
Wilberforce, OH   45384

Wilmington College
Wilmington, OH   45177

OKLAHOMA
Bacone College
Muskogee, OK   74403

Bartlesville Wesleyan
  College
2201 Silver-Lake Road
Bartlesville, OK   74006-6299

Bethany Nazarene College
6729 NW 39 Expressway
Bethany, OK   73008

Carl Albert Junior College
P.O. Box 606
Poteau, OK   74953

Connors State College
College Road
Warner, OK   74469

East Central University
Ada, OK   74820-6899

El Reno Junior College
P.O. Box 370
El Reno, OK   73036

Northern Oklahoma College
1220 East Grand Avenue
Tonkawa, OK   74653

Northwestern Oklahoma State
  University
Alva, OK   73717

Oklahoma City Community
  College
7777 South May Avenue
Oklahoma City, OK   73159

Oklahoma City University
NW 23rd and Blackwelder
Oklahoma City, OK   73106

Oklahoma State University
  Technical Institute
900 North Portland
Oklahoma City, OK   73107

Oral Roberts University
7777 South Lewis
Tulsa, OK   74171

Phillips University
University Station
Enid, OK   73702

Rose State College
6420 SE 15th Street
Midwest City, OK   73110

Southeastern Oklahoma State
  University
Durant, OK   74701

Opportunities for Credit

OKLAHOMA (cont.)
Southwestern Oklahoma State
University
Weatherford, OK   73096

University of Oklahoma
660 Parrington Oval
Norman, OK   73019

University of Science and
Arts of Oklahoma
Chickasha, OK   73018

Western Oklahoma State
College
2801 North Main Street
Altus, OK   73521

OREGON
Bassist College
2000 SW Fifth Avenue
Portland, OR   97201

Blue Mountain Community
College
P.O. Box 100
Pendleton, OR   97801-0100

Central Oregon Community
College
College Way
Bend, OR   97701

Chemeketa Community College
P.O. Box 14007
Salem, OR   97309-5008

Clackamas Community College
19600 Molalla Avenue
Oregon City, OR   97045

Clatsop Community College
16th and Jerome
Astoria, OR   97103

Eastern Oregon State College
La Grande, OR   97850

Judson Baptist College
400 East Scenic Drive
The Dalles, OR   97058

Lane Community College
4000 East 30th Avenue
Eugene, OR   97405

Lewis and Clark College
0615 Southwest Palatine Hill
Portland, OR   97219

Linfield College
McMinnville, OR   97128-6894

Marylhurst College for
Lifelong Learning
Marylhurst, OR   97036-0261

Mount Hood Community
College
26000 Southeast Stark
Gresham, OR   97030

Portland Community College
12000 Southwest 49th Avenue
Portland, OR   97219

Portland State University
P.O. Box 751
Portland, OR   97207

Umpqua Community College
P.O Box 967
Roseburg, OR   97470-0226

University of Portland
5000 N Willamette Boulevard
Portland, OR   97203-5798

Warner Pacific College
2219 Southeast 68th Avenue
Portland, OR   97215-4099

Western Conservative Baptist
Seminary
5511 SE Hawthorne Boulevard
Portland, OR   97215

PENNNSYLVANIA
Alliance College
Fullerton Avenue
Cambridge Springs, PA   16403

Alvernia College
Reading, PA   19607

Opportunities for Credit

Baptist Bible College of
Pennsylvania
538 Venard Road
Clarks Summit, PA 18411

Bucks County Community
College
Swamp Road
Newtown, PA 18940

Butler County Community
College
College Drive Oak Hills
Butler, PA 16001

Cabrini College
Eagle-King of Prussia Roads
Radnor, PA 19087

Chatham College
Woodland Road
Pittsburgh, PA 15232

Chestnut Hill College
Chestnut Hill
Philadelphia, PA 19118-2695

Clarion University of
Pennsylvania, Clarion
Clarion, PA 16214

Clarion University of
Pennsylvania, Venango
1801 West First Street
Oil City, PA 16301-3297

Community College of
Allegheny County, Allegheny
Campus
808 Ridge Avenue
Pittsburgh, PA 15212

Community College of
Allegheny County, South
Campus
1750 Clairton Road
West Mifflin, PA 15122

Curtis Institute of Music
1726 Locust Street
Philadelphia, PA 19103

Delaware County Community
College
Route 252 and Media Line
Road
Media, PA 19063

Delaware Valley College of
Science and Agriculture
Doylestown, PA 18901

Eastern College
Saint Davids, PA 19087

Elizabethtown College
Elizabethtown, PA 17022

Geneva College
College Avenue
Beaver Falls, PA 15010

Gettysburg College
Gettysburg, PA 17325-1486

Gratz College
10th Street and Tabor Road
Philadelphia, PA 19141

Grove City College
Grove City, PA 16127

Gwynedd-Mercy College
Sumneytown Pike
Gwynedd Valley, PA 19437

Harcum Junior College
Bryn Mawr, PA 19010-3476

Harrisburg Area Community
College
3300 Cameron Street Road
Harrisburg, PA 17110-2999

Indiana University of
Pennsylvania
Indiana, PA 15705

Lackawanna Junior College
901 Prospect Avenue
Scranton, PA 18505

La Roche College
9000 Babcock Boulevard
Pittsburgh, PA 15237-5828

Opportunities for Credit

PENNSYLVANIA (cont.)
Lebanon Valley College
Annville, PA 17003-0501

Lutheran Theological
Seminary, Gettysburg
61 West Confederate Avenue
Gettysburg, PA 17325

Lycoming College
Williamsport, PA 17701-5192

Mansfield University of
Pennsylvania
Mansfield, PA 16933

Marywood College
2300 Adams Avenue
Scranton, PA 18509-1598

Mercyhurst College
501 East 38th Street
Erie, PA 16546

Millersville University of
Pennsylvania
Millersville, PA 17551

Moravian College
Bethlehem, PA 18018

Mount Aloysius Junior
College
Cresson, PA 16630

Neumann College
Aston, PA 19014

Northeastern Christian
Junior College
1860 Montgomery Avenue
Villanova, PA 19085

Penn State, DuBois
College Place
Dubois, PA 15801

Point Park College
201 Wood Street
Pittsburgh, PA 15222

Reading Area Community
College
10 South Second Street
P.O. Box 1706
Reading, PA 19603

Saint Joseph's University
5600 City Avenue
Philadelphia, PA 19131

Seton Hill College
Greensburg, PA 15601

Slippery Rock University
Slippery Rock, PA
16057-9989

Spring Garden College
102 East Mermaid Lane
Chestnut Hill, PA 19119

Susquehanna University
University Avenue
Selinsgrove, PA 17870-9989

Temple University
Philadelphia, PA 19122

University of Pittsburgh,
Pittsburgh
Pittsburgh, PA 15260-0001

University of Pittsburgh,
Titusville
504 East Main Street
Titusville, PA 16354-2097

University of Scranton
Scranton, PA 18510

Valley Forge Christian
College
Charlestown Road
Phoenixville, PA 19460

Waynesburg College
51 West College Street
Waynesburg, PA 15370

West Chester University
University and High Street
West Chester, PA 19383

Opportunities for Credit

Westmoreland County
Community College
Youngwood, PA 15697-1895

Wilkes College
Box 111, 170 South Franklin
South
Wilkes-Barre, PA 18702

Williamsport Area Community
College
1005 West Third Street
Williamsport, PA 17701

Wilson College
Chambersburg, PA 17201

York College
Country Club Road
York, PA 17403-3426

RHODE ISLAND
Community College of Rhode
Island
400 East Avenue
Warwick, RI 02886

Johnson and Wales College
Abbott Park Place
Providence, RI 02903-3776

Roger Williams College
Old Ferry Road
Bristol, RI 02809

Salve Regina College
Ochre Point Avenue
Newport, RI 02840

SOUTH CAROLINA
Aiken Technical College
P.O. Drawer 696
Aiken, SC 29802-0696

Chesterfield-Marlboro
Technical College
Drawer 1007
Cheraw, SC 29520-1007

The Citadel
Charleston, SC 29409

Coker College
Hartsville, SC 29550

College of Charleston
Charleston, SC 29424

Columbia Bible College
P.O. Box 3122
Columbia, SC 29230-3122

Columbia College
Columbia College Drive
Columbia, SC 29203

Converse College
580 East Main Street
Spartanburg, SC 29301

Horry-Georgetown Technical
College
P.O. Box 1966
Conway, SC 29526

Lutheran Theological
Southern Seminary
4201 North Main Street
Columbia, SC 29203

Midlands Technical College
P.O. Box 2408
Columbia, SC 29202

Newberry College
2100 College
Newberry, SC 29108

South Carolina State College
Orangeburg, SC 29117

University of South
Carolina, Aiken
171 University Parkway
Aiken, SC 29801

University of South
Carolina, Coastal
Carolina College
P.O. Box 1954
Conway, SC 29526

University of South
Carolina, Union
P.O. Drawer 729
Union, SC 29379

SOUTH CAROLINA (cont.)
Williamsburg Technical
College
601 Lane Road
Kingstree, SC 29556

Winthrop College
Oakland Avenue
Rock Hill, SC 29733

SOUTH DAKOTA
Augustana College
29th and Summit
Sioux Falls, SD 57197

Black Hills State College
1200 University Street
Spearfish, SD 57783

Dakota State College
Madison, SD 57042

Mount Marty College
1105 West 8th Street
Yankton, SD 57078

National College
321 Kansas City Street
Rapid City, SD 57701

Presentation College
1500 North Main
Aberdeen, SD 57401-1299

Sioux Falls College
1501 South Prairie Avenue
Sioux Falls, SD 57105-1699

TENNESSEE
Austin Peay State University
College Street
Clarksville, TN 37040

Belmont College
1800 Belmont Boulevard
Nashville, TN 37203

Bethel College
Cherry Street
McKenzie, TN 38201

Bristol College
P.O. Box 757
Bristol, TN 37621-0757

Christian Brothers College
650 East Parkway South
Memphis, TN 38104

Cleveland State Community
College
P.O. Box 3570
Cleveland, TN 37320-3570

Columbia State Community
College
Hampshire Pike
Columbia, TN 38402-1315

Cumberland University
Lebanon, TN 37087

East Tennessee State
University
Johnson City, TN 37614-0002

Fisk University
17th Avenue North
Nashville, TN 37203

Free Will Baptist Bible
College
3606 West End Avenue
Nashville, TN 37205-2498

King College
Bristol, TN 37620

Memphis Academy of Arts
Overton Park
Memphis, TN 38112

Memphis State University
Memphis, TN 38152

Mid-South Bible College
P.O. Box 12144
Memphis, TN 38182-0144

Nashville State Technical
Institute
120 White Bridge Road
Nashville, TN 37209

Roane State Community
College
Harriman, TN 37748

Shelby State Community
College
P.O. Box 40568
Memphis, TN 38174-0568

Southern College of
Seventh-Day Adventists
Box 370
Collegedale, TN 37315-0370

State Technical Institute,
Memphis
5983 Macon Cove
Memphis, TN 38134

Tennessee Technological
University
Cookeville, TN 38505

Trevecca Nazarene College
333 Murfreesboro Road
Nashville, TN 37203-4411

Tusculum College
P.O. Box 5049
Greeneville, TN 37743-9997

University of the South
Sewanee, TN 37375-4013

University of Tennessee,
Knoxville
Knoxville, TN 37996-0154

University of Tennessee,
Martin
Martin, TN 38238-5009

Volunteer State Community
College
Nashville Pike
Gallatin, TN 37066-3188

TEXAS
Abilene Christian University
Abilene, Texas 79699

Amarillo College
P.O. Box 447
Amarillo, TX 79178

Amber University
1700 Eastgate Drive
Garland, TX 75041

American Technological
University
P.O. Box 1416 US Hwy 190
West
Killeen, TX 76540-1416

Austin College
900 North Grand
Sherman, TX 75090

Central Texas College
Highway 190 West
Killeen, TX 76541

Dallas Baptist University
7777 West Kiest Boulevard
Dallas, TX 75211-9800

Eastfield College
3737 Motley Drive
Mesquite, TX 75150-2099

East Texas Baptist
University
1209 North Grove Street
Marshall, TX 75670

East Texas State University,
Commerce
East Texas Station
Commerce, TX 75428

East Texas State University,
Texarkana
P.O. Box 5518
Texarkana, TX 75501

El Paso Community College
P.O Box 20500
El Paso, TX 79998

Hardin-Simmons University
2200 Hickory
Abilene, TX 79698

Hill Junior College
P.O. Box 619
Hillsboro, TX 76645

Houston Baptist University
7502 Fondren Road
Houston, TX 77074

Opportunities for Credit

TEXAS (cont.)
Howard County Junior College
1001 South Birdwell Lane
Big Spring, TX 79720-3799

Jacksonville College
Pine Street
Jacksonville, TX 75766

Lee College
P.O. Box 818
Baytown, TX 77522-0818

LeTourneau College
P.O. Box 7001
Longview, TX 75607

Lubbock Christian College
5601 West 19th
Lubbock, TX 79407

McLennan Community College
1400 College Drive
Waco, TX 76708

McMurry College
Sayles Boulevard & 14th
 Street
Abilene, TX 79697

Midwestern State University
3400 Taft Boulevard
Wichita Falls, TX 76308

Mountain View College
4849 West Illinois
Dallas, TX 75211-6599

Our Lady of the Lake
 University
411 SW 24th Street
San Antonio, TX 78285-0001

Panola Junior College
West Panola Street
Carthage, TX 75633

Saint Mary's University
One Camino Santa Maria
San Antonio, TX 78284-0400

San Jacinto College, Central
8060 Spencer Highway
Pasadena, TX 77505

Southwestern Adventist
 College
Keene, TX 76059

Southwestern Assemblies of
 God College
1200 Sycamore
Waxahachie, TX 75165

Southwestern University
University Avenue
Georgetown, TX 78626

Stephen F. Austin State
 University
1936 North Street
Nacogdoches, TX 75962

Texas A & I University
Santa Gertrudis
Kingsville, TX 78363

University of Dallas
University of Dallas Station
Irving, Texas 75061

University of Houston,
University Park
4800 Calhoun
Houston, TX 77004

University of Mary
 Hardin-Baylor
M H-B Station
Belton, TX 76513

University of Saint Thomas
3812 Montrose Boulevard
Houston, TX 77006

University of Texas, Dallas
P.O. Box 830688
Richardson, TX 75083-0688

Vernon Regional Junior
 College
4400 College Drive
Vernon, TX 76384

Weatherford College
308 East Park Avenue
Weatherford, TX 76086

Wharton County Junior College
911 Boling Highway
Wharton, TX   77488

UTAH
College of Eastern Utah
400 East 4th North
Price, UT   84501

Latter Day Saints Business
  College
411 East South Temple
Salt Lake City, UT   84111

Southern Utah State College
351 West Center
Cedar City, UT   84720

Utah Technical College,
  Provo
P.O. Box 1609
Provo, UT   84603

Weber State College
3950 Harrison Boulevard
Ogden, UT   84408-1011

Westminster College of Salt
  Lake City
1840 South 13th East
Salt Lake City, UT   84105

VERMONT
Burlington College
95 North Avenue
Burlington, VT   05401-8477

Castleton State College
Castleton, VT   05735

Goddard College
Plainfield, VT   05667

Johnson State College
Johnson, VT   05656

Lyndon State College
Lyndonville, VT   05851

Norwich University
Northfield, VT   05663

School for International
  Training
Kipling Road
Brattleboro, VT   05301

Southern Vermont College
Monument Road
Bennington, VT   05201

Trinity College
Colchester Avenue
Burlington, VT   05401

Vermont Technical College
Randolph Center, VT   05061

VIRGINIA
Averett College
420 West Main Street
Danville, VA   24541

Blue Ridge Community College
P.O. Box 80
Weyers Cave, VA 24486

Christopher Newport College
50 Shoe Lane
Newport News, VA   23606

Ferrum College
Ferrum, VA   24088-9001

George Mason University
4400 University Drive
Fairfax, VA   22030

Germanna Community College
P.O Box 339
Locust Grove, VA   22508

Hampton University
Hampton, VA   23668

James Madison University
Harrisonburg, VA   22807

John Tyler Community College
Drawer T
Chester, VA   23831-5399

Longwood College
Farmville, VA   23901

Opportunities for Credit

VIRGINIA (cont.)
Mary Baldwin College
Staunton, VA 24401

Mary Washington College
Fredericksburg, VA
22401-5358

Marymount College of Virginia
2807 North Glebe Road
Arlington, VA 22207

Norfolk State University
2401 Corprew Avenue
Norfolk, VA 23504

Northern Virginia Community
  College
4001 Wakefield Chapel Road
Annandale, VA 22003

Randolph-Macon College
Ashland, VA 23005-1698

Richard Bland College of the
  College of William and Mary
Route 1 Box 77-A
Petersburg, VA 23805

Southern Seminary Junior
  College
Buena Vista, VA 24416

Southwest Virginia Community
  College
Box S V C C
Richlands, VA 24641

Tidewater Community College
State Route 135
Portsmouth, VA 23703

University of Richmond
Richmond, VA 23173-1903

Virginia Commonwealth
  University
910 West Franklin Street
Richmond, VA 23284-0001

Virginia Highlands Community
  College
P.O. Box 828
Abingdon, VA 24210

Virginia Intermont College
Harmling Street
Bristol, VA 24201

Virginia State University
Petersburg, VA 23803

Virginia Wesleyan College
Wesleyan Drive
Norfolk, VA 23502-5599

WASHINGTON
Bellevue Community College
3000 Landerholm Circle SE
Bellevue, WA 98009-2037

Big Bend Community College
Andrews and 24th
Moses Lake, WA 98837

Clark College
1800 East McLoughlin
  Boulevard
Vancouver, WA 98663

Cornish Institute
710 East Roy
Seattle, WA 98102-4696

Eastern Washington University
Cheney, WA 99004

Grays Harbor College
Aberdeen, WA 98520-7599

Green River Community College
12401 South East 320
Auburn, WA 98002

Highline Community College
240th and Pacific Highway S
Midway, WA 98032-0424

Lower Columbia College
Longview, WA 98632

North Seattle Community
  College
9600 College Way North
Seattle, WA 98103

Olympic College
16th & Chester
Bremertown, WA 98310-1699

List of Institutions

Pacific Lutheran University
Tacoma, WA 98447-003

Saint Martin's College
700 College Street Southeast
Lacey, WA 98503

Seattle Central Community
  College
1701 Broadway
Seattle, WA 98122

Skagit Valley College
2405 College Way
Mount Vernon, WA 98273

Tacoma Community College
5900 South 12th Street
Tacoma, WA 98465

Walla Walla Community College
500 Tausick Way
Walla Walla, WA 99362

Washington State University
Pullman, WA 99164-1036

Whatcom Community College
5217 Northwest Road
Bellingham, WA 98226

Yakima Valley Community
  College
16th & Nob Hill Boulevard
Yakima, WA 98902

WEST VIRGINIA
Concord College
Athens, WV 24712

Fairmont State College
Locust Avenue
Fairmont, WV 26554

Glenville State College
200 High Street
Glenville, WV 26351-9990

Marshall University
Huntington, WV 25701

Shepherd College
Shepherdstown, WV 25443

Southern West Virginia
  Community College
Box 2900
Logan, WV 25601-2900

University of Charleston
2300 MacCorkle Avenue SE
Charleston, WV 25304-1099

West Liberty State College
West Liberty, WV 26074

West Virginia Northern
  Community College
College Square
Wheeling, WV 26003

West Virginia State College
Institute, WV 25112

West Virginia University
Morgantown, WV 26506

West Virginia Wesleyan
  College
Buckhannon, WV 26201

Wheeling College
Wheeling, WV 26003

WISCONSIN
  Beloit College
  Beloit, WI 53511

Cardinal Stritch College
6801 North Yates Road
Milwaukee, WI 53217

Carroll College
100 North East Avenue
Waukesha, WI 53186

Gateway Technical Institute
1001 Main Street
Racine, WI 53403

Lakeland College
P.O Box 359
Sheboygan, WI 53081

Marian College
45 South National Avenue
Fond du Lac, WI 54935-4699

Opportunities for Credit

WISCONSIN (cont.)
Milwaukee Area Technical
College
1015 North 6th Street
Milwaukee, WI 53203

Mount Mary College
2900 Menomonee River Parkway
Milwaukee, WI 53222

Mount Senario College
College Avenue West
Ladysmith, WI 54848

Nicolet College and Technical
Institute
Box 518
Rhinelander, WI 54501

North Central Technical
Institute
1000 Campus Drive
Wausau, WI 54401

Northeast Wisconsin Technical
Institute
2740 West Mason Street
P.O. Box 19042
Green Bay, WI 54307-9042

Northland College
1411 Ellis Avenue
Ashland, WI 54806-3999

Saint Francis Seminary,
School of Pastoral Ministry
3257 South Lake Drive
Milwaukee, WI 53207-0905

Saint Norbert College
De Pere, WI 54115

Silver Lake College
2406 South Alverno Road
Manitowoc, WI 54220-9319

University of Wisconsin,
Green Bay
Green Bay, WI 54301-7001

University of Wisconsin,
LaCrosse
1725 State Street
LaCrosse, WI 54601

University of Wisconsin,
Madison
500 Lincoln Drive
Madison, WI 53706

University of Wisconsin,
Milwaukee
P.O. Box 413
Milwaukee, WI 53201

University of Wisconsin,
Platteville
725 West Main Street
Platteville, WI 53818-9998

University of Wisconsin,
Stevens Point
Stevens Point, WI 54481

University of Wisconsin,
Superior
1800 Grand Avenue
Superior, WI 54880-2898

Viterbo College
815 South 9th Street
LaCrosse, WI 54601

Waukesha County Technical
Institute
800 Main Street
Pewaukee, WI 53072

Western Wisconsin Technical
Institute
6th and Vine Streets
LaCrosse, WI 54601

Wisconsin Indianhead
Technical Institute
P.O. Box B
Shell Lake, WI 54871

WYOMING
Casper College
125 College Drive
Casper, WY 82601

Central Wyoming College
2660 Peck Avenue
Riverton, WY 82501-1520

Opportunities for Credit

Laramie County Community
  College
1400   East   College   Drive
Cheyenne, WY   82007-3299

University of Wyoming
Box 3434 University Station
Laramie, WY   82071

PUERTO RICO
  Antillian College
  Box 118
  Mayaguez, PR   00709-0118

Humacao University College
CUH Station
Humacao, PR   00661

Turabo University
P.O. Box 1091
Caguas, PR   00625

QUESTIONS	*Goddard College Off-Campus Study* Plainfield, VT 05667	*Empire State College Center For Distance Learning* 2 Union Avenue Saratoga Springs, NY 12866
What degrees can I earn in the program? Some independent learning colleges award only one degree. Others offer several.	Bachelor's and Master's degrees	Associate, Bachelor's and Master's degrees
What can I study in the program? Each independent learning program offers degrees in specific areas. Some also offer "general" or "interdisciplinary" degrees that allow you to study a wide range of topics from many disciplines.	Leadership and Management, Education, Psychology, Environmental Sciences, and Interdisciplinary Creative and Liberal Arts	Business, Human Services, Interdisciplinary Studies
What are the requirements for entrance into the program? Some independent learning programs require a high school diploma or equivalency; others do not. In addition, because of the special challenge of independent study, some programs require evidence of the ability to study on your own.	High School Diploma or Equivalency; Evidence of commitment to and basic ability for self-direction.	High School Diploma or Equivalency
Can I study part-time? Some programs allow part-time study. Others do not.	Full-time Study Only	Full- or Part-time Study
How long does each semester last? From 12 to 24 weeks, depending on the program. Some programs allow you to study at your own pace, with no semesters at all.	20-week semesters; 15 semester hours of advancement	16-week semesters
How do I get credit for my previous learning? Like many college programs for adults, independent learning colleges award credit for previous learning in a number of ways: transfer credit from other colleges; national standardized exams; apprentice, military and other training; and individual "life experience" portfolios.	Transfer Credits, Portfolios, Assessment, and Accepted Exams for Bachelor's degrees; Bachelor's degree required for M.A. study.	Transfer Credits, Exams, Military Education, and Approved Training Programs
How much of my degree can I earn through my previous learning? Each program is different, and all credits are subject to university requirements. Please keep in mind that very few students earn the maximum amounts listed here.	Up to 25% in portfolio assessment and up to 75% in transfer credit, but no more than 75% of a bachelor's degree in all	Up to 62% of an Associate or 75% of a Bachelor's degree.
How are independent study "courses" put together? Some programs have pre-set, carefully structured learning materials designed for adult independent study. In other programs, you and an instructor design an individualized study "contract" or plan just for you.	Individual Study Plans	Pre-set Materials
Independent study sounds lonely. How will I keep in touch with my professors and my fellow students? There's no doubt—these programs are for people with the discipline to study on their own. But each program provides ways to keep you in touch with counselors and instructors and, often, your fellow students.	Each semester begins with a 9-day stay at the Goddard campus in Vermont. There you meet with your advisor and make contact with other students. For the rest of the semester, you correspond regularly with your advisor.	Students work through their course materials under the guidance of a faculty member maintaining regular contact by phone or mail.
How much does each program cost? Each is different, and much depends on whether you are studying full- or part-time. REMEMBER: Union and company tuition benefits can help a great deal with tuition costs.	$2150 per semester for undergraduate work; $2400 per semester for Master's study	$57.00 per credit. (Most courses are 4 or 8 credits.)

Provided courtesy of CAEL (Council for Adult and Experiential Learning)

American Open University of New York Institute of Technology Central Islip, NY 11722	The Union for Experimenting Colleges and Universities Undergraduate Studies 632 Vine Street Suite 1010 Cincinnati, OH 45202	Regents College of the University of the State of New York Cultural Education Center Albany, NY 12230	Ohio University External Student Program 309 Tupper Hall Athens, OH 45701	Thomas A. Edison State College 101 West State Street Trenton, NJ 08625
Bachelor's degree	All Degrees from Bachelor's through Doctoral	Associate and Bachelor's degrees	Associate and Bachelor's degrees	Associate and Bachelor's degrees
Business Administration, General Studies and Behavioral Sciences, with options in Mental Health, Psychology, Sociology, and Criminal Justice	Business, Behavioral Sciences, Human Services, Health Care, and a wide range of Liberal Arts	Computers, Business, Electronics, Nuclear Technology, Nursing, and a wide range of Liberal Arts and Sciences	Associate degrees in Security and Safety Technology and a wide range of Liberal Arts and Sciences; Bachelor's degree in General Studies	Business and Management, The Liberal Arts, Applied Science and Technology, Human and Social Services, Nursing
High School Diploma or Equivalency	High School Diploma or Equivalency; Evidence of motivation and sense of educational responsibility	No Entrance Requirements; Students must be self-directed.	High School Diploma or Equivalency	No Entrance Requirements
Full- or Part-time Study	Full-time Only	Full- or Part-time Study	Full- or Part-time Study	Full- or Part-time Study
You have up to 6 months to complete any course but can register for new courses at any time.	13-week quarters	No Set Semesters	No Set Semesters	No Set Semesters
Transfer Credits, Exams, Military Education, Approved Training Programs, and Portfolio Assessment	Transfer Credits, Exams, Military Education, Approved Training Programs, and Portfolio Assessment	Transfer Credits, Exams, Military Education, Approved Training Programs, and Special Assessment	Transfer Credits, Exams, Military Education, Approved Training Programs, and Portfolio Assessment	Transfer Credits, Exams, Military Education, Approved Training Programs, Media-assisted instruction, Portfolio Assessment
Up to 90% of a Bachelor's degree	Up to 75% of a Bachelor's degree	No Limit	Up to 100% of an Associate or Bachelor's degree through portfolio assessment and other appropriate credit	No Limit
Pre-set Materials	Individualized Learning Contracts	Varied Methods	Pre-set Materials	Varied Methods
Students correspond with their professors by mail. In addition, a special computer conferencing system enables students to "talk" with their professors and fellow students.	In addition to its central faculty in Cincinnati, UECU has faculty members in your region with whom you meet regularly to plan and discuss your work.	Regents College has no classes. By mail or phone, your advisor helps you identify educational resources that, together with your previous learning, enable you to earn a degree. The Graduate Resource Network gives you local support and help.	Correspondence courses include a textbook and study guide. The lessons you do are submitted to OU faculty for grading and feedback. In addition, midterm and final exams are taken with OU proctors in your local area.	Edison College has no classes. You are encouraged to stay in touch with advisors by mail or phone. An advisement center is available. Nursing Program has Peer Study Groups. Staff and workshops are available for special college programs.
$50 application fee; $100 matriculation fee; $75 per credit	$1300 per quarter	$225 enrollment fee; $125-175 per year records fee; $60 graduation fee; you pay for courses and exams directly	$50 admission fee; $35 matriculation fee per year; $31 per quarter hour for correspondence course and $17 per quarter hour for exam credit; $5 enrollment fee per course	$50 application fee; $125 (NJ) - $200 (others) First Year Tuition Equivalency Fee; $100 (NJ) - $150 (others) Subsequent Year's Tuitition Equivalency Fee; $70 Graduation Fee

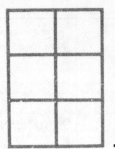

Index

A.

About CAEL

The Council for Adult and Experiential Learning (CAEL) is a non-profit national association of institutions, agencies and individuals dedicated to fostering quality experiential learning and the valid and reliable assessment of its outcomes. Presently there are more than 500 institutional and individual members in the United States, Canada and Puerto Rico.

Experiential Learning refers to learning in which the learner is directly in touch with the realities being studied. CAEL sponsors research, publications, conferences, and professional staff development activities.

In support of adult learners, CAEL has assisted in the development of microcomputer-assisted guidance, counseling, and educational planning programs. CAEL has also published a number of student guides.

About the Author

Susan Simosko, at the time of the first printing of this publication was the Director of Testing and Assessment at Thomas A. Edison State College in New Jersey. There she helped adults who are self-motivated learners to earn college credit for what they have learned outside the college classroom. Currently, Ms. Simosko is the Director of Communications for CAEL. She is a frequent speaker at national conferences and workshops.